APR 18 1996

"DIAL B FOR BIRDER!"

Lola Oberman

D1417389

NORTHWORD
PRESS, INC
Box 1360, Minocqua, WI 54548

DEDICATION

To Steve,
who understands about birders—
and deadlines

© 1992 Lola Oberman
Published by:
NorthWord Press, Inc.
P.O. Box 1360
Minocqua, WI 54548

ISBN 1-55971-186-8

Edited by Greg Linder
Designed by Russell S. Kuepper
Cover art by Bruce Cochran
Interior illustrations by Mary Shafer

For a free catalog describing NorthWord's line of books
and gift items, call toll free 1-800-336-5666.

Library of Congress Cataloging-in-Publication Data

Oberman, Lola
    Dial B for birder / by Lola Oberman
      p. cm.
    ISBN 1-55971-186-8 : $12.95
    1. Oberman, Lola. 2. Bird watchers--Washington Metropolitan Area-
-Biography. 3. Birds--United States--Identification. 4. Audubon
Naturalist Society of the Central Atlantic States. I. Title.
QL31.024A3 1992
598'.07234753--dc20
                                                      92-26362
                                                         CIP

CONTENTS

ON CALL

From the garden I hear the telephone. Three rings, a brief silence, then comes the familiar shout:

"Bird call!"

Any hour of the day, any day of the year, I can expect these interruptions whenever I'm within earshot of the telephone. When I'm away, my answering machine picks up the messages. The calls, averaging about 200 a year, are as varied as the birds that fly, revealing an endless curiosity about the world of birds.

It was our son, Steve, when he was at home, who started summoning me to the telephone in that manner. "Bird call!" he would sing out, half-amused and, I think, half-impressed, having a limited knowledge of birds himself. Now, it's my husband who picks up the phone. He could answer most of the questions himself, but Ted defers to me on the logical grounds that it was I, not he, who volunteered to perform this public service under the auspices of the Audubon Naturalist Society.

When I joined the ranks of the Society's home volunteers I had no idea of the commitment I was making. I expected only occasional calls, say two or three a month, from people in the metropolitan area of Washington, D.C., where I live. But before long I was fielding calls daily, some from distant points.

Times have changed. In the beginning there were ten of us, known as "telephone identifiers" because most of the calls referred to us by the Society's headquarters in Chevy Chase, Maryland, had to do with bird identification, raising questions that the administrative staff had neither the time nor the expertise to handle. Now that some of the original corps members have dropped out or moved from the area, only three of us are left to handle an increasing number of calls. It's not only that the population of the Washington area has grown during those years; the interest in birdwatching has also grown at a phenomenal rate. And long-distance telephoning is used more casually these days. I am no longer surprised to find that I'm talking to an enthusiast in Florida or New Jersey or Ohio.

How these distant callers got my name and phone number was for a long while a mystery, until it occurred to me to ask one of them. It was the young man from Corpus Christi, Texas, who explained it to me. He was very excited; I was very anxious. I had turned off the broiler, hoping dinner wouldn't be ruined while I listened to him. His excitement was understandable. He was convinced that he had discovered a new species—or at least a new subspecies—of the great-tailed grackle, and he gave a meticulous description of a great-tailed grackle, normally all black, which had one striking aberration: Its outer tail feathers were white!

His discovery was something less than earthshaking. I had observed the same kind of marking on a common grackle in my back yard, two years in a row. It was merely a case of partial albinism, not at all uncommon in the bird world.

Sorry to disillusion the enthusiast, I broke the news as kindly as I could, all the while pondering his initial remark, "I thought I ought to report . . ." But why report to me?

He thought the Audubon Society would want to know—and he figured that the Audubon Society, like all important agencies, was located in Washington. So he got the number from the Washington information operator and was referred to me. Suddenly I saw the light. All those callers from remote places had followed the same procedure—and Information, checking the alphabetical listing, did not think to look under "N" for National Audubon Society, but found under "A" the Audubon Naturalist Society—a local organization whose geographic scope is the Central Atlantic States.

It was humbling—and amusing—to learn that for all this time I had been accepted by so many birdwatchers as the official voice of National Audubon. But what did it matter? They got the information they sought and the feeling that someone in Washington was listening to them.

As the number of calls has increased, so too has the variety of questions. I no longer think of myself as a mere "identifier"; I have become a sort of "Dear Abby" specializing in birds. Even so, more than half of the callers are seeking help in identification, and I have learned that identifying birds from a telephone description is not an easy matter. It requires, besides a knowledge of birds, a great deal of patience, a genuine desire to be helpful, the ability to listen carefully for clues, and the capacity to ask the right questions to elicit further clues. And it requires a certain imaginative insight to offset the misperceptions of inexpert observers and to interpret their imprecise, unscientific descriptions, for most of the callers are amateurs with little or no vocabulary for describing bird anatomy. They often lack any concept of classification that could be helpful in placing an unknown bird in its proper family.

The man who asks, "What's that funny woodpecker that dives into the water?" isn't talking about a woodpecker at all, but about a kingfisher. But another caller is definitely talking about a woodpecker when he speaks of "a big, black, crow-like bird with a red topknot and racing stripes down its neck." Amateurish as the description is, it does present a graphic impression of the pileated woodpecker, which is fairly common in our area.

This dramatic, flashy woodpecker is often mistaken for the renowned ivory-billed woodpecker, which has not been seen in these parts since the days of John James Audubon and is now considered virtually extinct. There was a great flurry of excitement in 1987 when ornithologists discovered the ivory-billed in Cuba. But I get regular reports of ivory-bills from confident amateurs in suburban Washington who can't be dissuaded from their conviction that they have made a great discovery. One woman insisted that she had "a whole family of ivory-billed woodpeckers" eating at her suet feeder in Arlington, Virginia. It is useless, I've learned, to argue with people who are so assured of their rightness.

Over the years I've developed a series of questions to ask as aids to identification:

"*Where did you see the bird?*" Geographical location can be important. It makes a difference whether the bird was seen in the mountains of western Maryland or Virginia or on the Atlantic coast. Habitat is a vital clue. Is it a bird of city parks, of woodland or open fields, of sandy beaches or rocky cliffs or wetlands?

"*Did you see it with binoculars?*" This is a dual-purpose question. It helps determine how well the bird was actually perceived and at the same time gives some indication of the observer's level of expertise. Many people who are moderately interested in birds don't even own binoculars.

This leads to the questions: "*How close was it?*" and "*How long did you observe it?*" A five-second glimpse of a bird flying over the highway seen from a car going 55 miles per hour is a lost cause.

"*When?*" is an important consideration. It is natural, but not always safe, to assume that the sighting was recent. I recall puzzling for some time over a description that certainly sounded like a barn swallow—but a barn swallow in the District of Columbia in mid-January is highly improbable. Belatedly, the caller mentioned that he'd been wondering about that bird ever since seeing it last summer at his cottage, where it had built a nest on the porch.

Time of day, too, is significant because lighting conditions affect perception, especially of color. Was it seen by dawn's early light, at dusk, or at high noon?

All of this is background information. Now comes the tricky part—descriptive details. For starters:

"*How big was the bird?*" Size is not only critical to correct identification; it is also the element that is most subject to error. When a man tells me he was driving down a country lane and saw "a huge, six-foot bird standing by the roadside," I conclude that he is either visually handicapped, subject to hallucinations, or under the influence of alcohol, and probably shouldn't be driving, even on country roads. In any case, his testimony can't be accepted literally.

This is an extreme example. But I've learned that few people can give reasonably reliable estimates of size in actual measurements. So I ask for comparisons with familiar birds. "How big in relation to a robin?" seems safe enough, but even that doesn't guarantee an accurate response. Inexperienced observers don't remember sizes well, and they may not be familiar with even the most common species. One cannot assume.

I recall, in trying to identify a hawk, asking the question, "How big in relation to a crow?"

Oh, much bigger than a crow, the caller assured me; at least three times as big. I was totally baffled until he added helpfully, "It was more the size of the ravens I see along the road."

But we don't have ravens around here. The birds he called ravens were crows; the birds he called crows were common grackles. So we were back to a crow-sized hawk after all.

Confronted with a real puzzle, I often solve it by casting out the size estimate as completely unreliable and speculating on what a bird with the given field marks would be if it were half (or twice) the specified size.

From size, we get down to the specifics of color, general shape, type of beak, length of tail, feeding behavior, manner of flight, and song or call if any (and if it can be described or imitated). All of these can be helpful, but one or two distinctive traits may establish the identity rather quickly without going through the whole checklist of questions. A bird with a melodious song, singing nonstop for an hour in the middle of the night, can only be a mockingbird. A large flock of "golden-appearing birds with crests" feeding on holly berries has to be cedar waxwings. "A shiny black bird with a brown head" is unmistakably a brown-headed cowbird.

Those are the easy ones. But there are many species with subtler distinguishing traits that are discerned only by the sophisticated eye, among them all sorts of sparrows and hawks and look-alike sandpipers, not to mention the females and immatures of many well-known species. Who would expect a *scarlet* tanager to appear in yellowish-green garb? Or an *indigo* bunting in sober brown?

Added to that, there are occasional birds in aberrant plumage, albinistic or melanistic. A "black bird with a long tail like a grackle that looks as if he's wearing white spectacles" turns out to be exactly that: a grackle with albinistic markings. And "a lovely, pale-beige bird, the size of a robin" traveling with a flock of robins is obviously an albino robin.

Escaped cage birds are not unusual, especially in residential areas. I've had parakeets feeding with house sparrows on the Mall that stretches from the grounds of the Washington Monument to Capitol Hill; a Brazilian cardinal in a park adjacent to the Watergate apartments; a golden pheasant from Asia strolling through the back yards of suburban Bethesda; a bar-headed goose from Egypt floating serenely on the lake adjacent to Dulles Airport; and a spotted munia from India braving the cold of a winter day in Rockville, Maryland. ("I swear, I am not hallucinating," said the woman. "It's an all-black bird with white polka-dots on its breast.")

Fortunately, the newer field guides show all these species (and others) in a section titled "Exotics." But there are finches and other small tropical birds from the Caribbean that I have never sorted out. ("Tell them you don't do cage birds," Ted suggests from the sidelines.)

Some birds, in spite of all efforts, seem destined to remain mysteries. But I don't easily tolerate mysteries. Rather than give up on an intriguing bird, I may, if time and distance permit, decide to go and see it myself, suspecting that it has been poorly observed or inadequately described. Always there is the alluring possibility, of course, that this is a rarity from another continent or climate that will make ornithological history—and indeed this has happened more than once. One year, within a month, there was a scissor-tailed flycatcher from the Southwest catching insects on Antietam Battlefield and a long-billed curlew from the Great Plains feeding on crickets on a football field in Brandywine, Maryland.

Knowing that these things happen, I may make a quick decision to jump in the car and track down the mystery bird. It may, if I succeed in finding it (for birds can't be expected to stay in the same spot), turn out to be nothing more unusual than a female house finch or a song sparrow, but at least my curiosity and that of the caller is satisfied.

· · ·

Ranking second to identification questions are feeder questions, an indication that more and more people have become interested in attracting birds to their back yards. Squirrels are the recurrent theme. I hail the ingenuity that has produced guaranteed squirrel-proof feeders; but I also hail the ingenuity of squirrels. I'm confident that they will never be totally bested by humans.

Pest birds, too, are a constant problem: "How can I keep starlings away from the suet feeder?" and "How can I attract chickadees and titmice without attracting house finches?" But there are also questions about when to start and stop the feeding season; what formula to use for hummingbird feeders and how often to change it; and whether birds can become too dependent on backyard feeding stations and forget to migrate.

All these reflect a genuine concern for the well-being of the birds. Other questions reflect a desire to understand bird behavior. Why do birds start singing at dawn? What are they saying? Why do mockingbirds sing at night? Why would mockingbirds be doing a courtship dance in November? (This is not a courtship dance; these are rivals competing for winter feeding territory.) Why is this crazy cardinal bashing his head against my bedroom window? (He's confusing his reflection with a real-life competitor.)

There are birds-in-distress calls, especially in the spring and early summer when young birds fall from nests. But there are also birds that are temporarily stunned after hitting windows, birds that are struck by cars, and birds that have been mauled by cats. In our area we are fortunate to have a network of volunteers who are trained and licensed to give care to injured birds, and I refer many SOS calls to them.

Idle curiosity prompts a fair number of calls each year. I put in the "Trivia Quiz" category such questions as:

What is the smallest bird in the world?

What is the life span of the bald eagle?

Do birds sneeze?

Many such calls are the result, I suspect, of a dull day at the office when colleagues get into desultory conversation and, occasionally, argument. That was the background of a call from Baltimore (during office hours) that began: "I'm sure you have weightier matters to deal with, but a friend and I have a small wager and we'd like you to settle it, if you have the time."

The question was: "How fast can a wild turkey fly?" There is something to be learned even from trivial questions. I turned to John R. Terres' *The Audubon Encyclopedia of North American Birds*, as I often do in seeking answers to esoteric questions, and relayed the information that wild turkeys have been timed at flight speeds up to 55 miles per hour. It surprised me as much as it did my caller to learn that the ungainly turkey is capable of such speed.

With the rapid increase of serious birders in the field (the U.S. Fish and Wildlife Service estimates seven million in the United

States), I get more requests for guidance these days: Where is the best nearby location from which to watch the hawk migration? When do the swans start coming in at Blackwater Refuge? What is the best spot for finding migrant warblers? Where can I find a sharp-tailed sparrow (or a prairie warbler, or evening grosbeak, or ruffed grouse)? It is extremely satisfying to be able to guide an eager birder to a special bird that will be added to a life list.

Visitors from out of town often call to ask directions to local birding hotspots or for information about guided field trips. Local birders planning trips to remote spots call to ask if I know of birding opportunities in Texas, or California, or Arizona, or Manitoba. It is always a pleasure to share experiences, trip lists, and the literature we've accumulated in our birding travels.

The best calls are those that pose no questions at all; their sole purpose is to share observations of birds and their fascinating behavior. A man calls to share his delight in finding barn swallows nesting in an electric light fixture on his porch. A woman in northwest Washington, breathless with excitement, calls to tell me of a flock of 200 snow geese flying low, right over her apartment. She has never seen such a sight before and she is impelled to share it with someone. The same impulse inspires a schoolgirl who has watched an enormous flock of chimney swifts disappear into a smokestack, as if pulled in by a giant vacuum.

It is in this spirit of sharing that I have recorded here some of the memorable experiences with birds and with people that have come to me as a reward for keeping my telephone line open to all callers. The rewards have been many. I answer the telephone with a sense of anticipation, knowing that this call may lead to an adventure afield, a new avenue of absorbing research, a new friend, or a chain of reminiscences that will set this day apart from the ordinary.

❖

VOICES OF SPRING

It is the season of departures and arrivals here on the Atlantic Flyway. Geography is relative. This is south to the great flocks of waterfowl that come down for the winter, and for the siskins and juncos and white-throated sparrows in our back yard. Now they leave us . . .

It is north for the herons and egrets, the swallows and songbirds that have spent the winter in warmer climates. We welcome them back as we bid farewell to the honored guests of winter and hail the transients that are just passing through.

Out in the fields, the high clear notes of the meadowlark are heard above the clamor of northbound Canada geese stopping en route to feed and rest. Over the river, the chilling cry of a loon drowns the soft twitter of swallows swooping low over the water. In the back yard, the first robin joins the chorus of resident cardinals, chickadees, doves, and titmice, and the amorous gargle of the red-bellied woodpecker.

And the telephone rings . . .

THE IDES OF MARCH

Rustling gusts of wind announced the Ides of March in the early morning hours. By dawn the yard was full of tree debris and empty of birds. Mid-morning brought snow flurries out of purple skies, and noon brought a brief interlude of sunshine before a gray pall settled in.

Telephone calls were as varied as the weather.

There were worriers. "Where are all the birds? Why aren't there any birds at my feeder?"

It's a normal complaint on a windy day when birds hunker down in sheltered spots, waiting out the gale.

There were two identification requests, both reasonably easy to resolve from the descriptions. The "nondescript streaky gray bird" was surely a female house finch, and the dull, olive-green one with black and white wings was a goldfinch in winter dress, both common enough.

The only unusual call came from a plaintive woman who began, without introduction: "I'm not getting any orioles at my feeder."

"Neither am I," I replied, and before I could continue with the explanation that orioles are not common feeder visitors here, especially in March, she went on. "I put out orange halves and chopped apple, just like the book says, but I still don't get any orioles."

She showed remarkable resistance to the logic that you can't attract birds to your feeder if they aren't in the vicinity. She had read of orioles visiting feeders regularly, but she didn't remember where or when.

"Probably not in Maryland in March," I said. Orioles, both northern and orchard, have been tallied on Christmas Bird Counts occasionally, but never in great numbers; and now and

16

then a lone straggler that failed to migrate south shows up at a local feeder.

She sighed over her wasted generosity and hung up.

It was late afternoon before the telephone rang again, this time with a message of real interest. A woman living in a new sub-development in "up-county" farmland had seen a flock of eight "tall white birds" in a nearby field. She thought they must be cranes of some kind.

Visions of wood storks raced through my head. Eight wood storks this far north could establish ornithological history.

"Are they all white?" I asked.

"As far as I can see."

"Do they have long legs?"

"I'm sure they do because they're so tall. I can't really see their legs. They're just over a rise."

Other possibilities occurred to me. Great egrets, this early? Ibis? Pelicans? Any of these would be rare, and a flock of eight would be phenomenal.

I asked for the exact location and persuaded Ted that it was worth a half-hour trip, even in rush-hour traffic, and we were soon headed north on the interstate. The wind had abated and there were some promising breaks in the clouds by the time we arrived at the described location.

We drove past a row of new houses and parked where the road ended, overlooking the pleasant, rolling terrain of undisturbed farmland. From this vantage point, we quickly spotted the eight birds in mid-field, just over the crest, their long white necks outlined against the clouded sky.

We didn't need to set up our scope to identify them. Binoculars were quite adequate.

We looked at each other in disappointment and chagrin. We had traveled all that distance to see a small group of tundra swans, resting on their northward journey, not exactly a common sight this far inland, but common enough along the Chesapeake

Bay, especially on the eastern shore where flocks in the hundreds can be seen in winter.

After the first shock, we began to laugh. Eight tundra swans! What was that to two people who had seen 6,000 at a time?

The memory was still fresh. Only two weeks had passed since that magic day when we had stood speechless with wonder at the incredible sight of flock after flock of majestic swans dropping from the sky into a brown stubblefield, spreading across it like a drift of snow.

As seasoned birders are prone to do, we each made a mental count of the descending birds, and when they had all come to rest in that way-station on the flyway, we compared estimates. Six thousand swans! Who would believe there were that many on the entire continent?

We had made one last trip to the eastern shore as a final salute to winter, hoping to see the trailing edge of the great waterfowl migration before all the ducks and geese and swans had departed. Such numbers as these we had never envisioned. By a miracle of timing and chance, we had arrived at a vast staging center where swans from various points along the coast gathered in a great congregation on the first leg of their long trek to the Arctic.

In the field they regrouped, walked about conversing with one another, and rested. We watched in fascination for 20 minutes or more, and as we watched, snow geese, too, began to come in, a hundred or more at a time. The field was alive with activity.

We moved on reluctantly. When we returned four hours later, the field was deserted.

We thought then that we had seen the last of the swans for the season. But now we had been granted one more opportunity, a chance for a last farewell. Aren't eight swans better than none? The world is full of people who have never seen a single one.

Among them was the excited woman who had discovered them from her kitchen window. From that same window she saw us parked at the end of the road and drove down to join us. After introductions, we gave her the verdict: "These are tundra swans—the ones that used to be called whistling swans."

She couldn't have been happier if we had said they were wood storks.

For her benefit, we set up the scope for a better view. Her reactions were thoroughly rewarding. She exclaimed over their grace and beauty and treated them as a great rarity—a species she had known only in pictures and stories and had never hoped to see in the wild, certainly not within sight of her own home.

She was full of questions. Where did they come from? Where were they going? How long would they stay here?

She could scarcely believe that they would actually fly as far as 3,000 miles to build their nests, raise their young, and then make the return flight in the fall.

As we talked, rain began to fall in large drops, not a bone-chilling rain like yesterday's, but almost warm with the promise of spring. The sun found an opening in the clouds to the west; its rays illuminated the bright crystal splashes that pelted us as we said hasty good-byes and dashed for our cars.

Through the spattered windshield we could still see the swans, standing erect and alert on the horizon, unruffled by the sudden shower.

Then it was over. We stepped out into the warm, moist air and inhaled the earthy, after-shower aroma. To the west all was clear as the sun sank lower. To the east a brilliant rainbow appeared against the milky gray clouds, then above it a second rainbow, equally brilliant, two perfect arches stretching across the sky.

For minutes we watched as the colors deepened, then paled and slowly dissolved.

When we turned for a final look at the swans, they, too, had disappeared. Rush hour was over by the time we turned south on the interstate.

✜

DIAGNOSTIC SYMPTOMS OF BIRDWATCHER ADDICTION

The first awakening of an interest in birds is marvelous to behold, or, as so often happens in my case, to *hear* in an excited voice on the telephone. The experienced ear can detect the diagnostic symptoms of impending addiction.

When I hear the telltale note of wonder and delight, I feed the fever, giving unabashed encouragement to take the next step toward what may well become an unshakable lifelong habit.

When a hesitant caller (usually sounding apologetic) says, "I was referred to you by the Audubon Society," I can always hope for a report of a rare bird in the area. But this seldom happens. The bird in question usually turns out to be one of our everyday species, but the call may present an uncommon opportunity nevertheless.

So it happened one day when a young man with that familiar, apologetic tone, called to ask about a bird in his back yard. He had recently moved to a new development up-county, where there are still woods and open spaces, and he had begun putting out seeds for the birds.

"I don't really know anything about birds," he said, with an engaging humility. "Oh, I know cardinals and blue jays and that kind of thing. But I'm seeing birds I've never seen before, right by my window."

There was the first hint of a possible convert. Anyone who becomes interested enough in a bird to look up the number of the Audubon Society and call for help in identification has already taken the first step.

Apparently he had observed this little bird very closely and with more than casual interest, for he managed to give an excellent description of a Carolina chickadee, one of the commonest feeder visitors in the area. Yet he had never heard of it before.

"Let me write that down," he said, revealing the second symptom. Already he was beginning a list!

Encouraged, he dared to describe another bird, "smaller than an ordinary sparrow, brownish, with red on the top of its head that stops at the back of the neck, and more red just above the tail . . ."

He had gone far enough. I could tell him this was a house finch. He had seen several of them, he said, and I refrained from telling him he might soon have more than he cared to feed. But I *should* have told him, as he wrote down the No. 2 bird on his list, to listen for their delightful song.

There was still another bird, he confided, if I had the time. Again he sounded hesitant. "I'm afraid they all sound quite a bit alike," he said. "This one also has a grayish back, like the chickadee, and a white front, and a black cap. But it has a longer beak, quite sharp, and a very short tail."

This novice was a careful observer. He had given all the clues I needed.

"Does it walk upside down on tree trunks?" I asked.

"Yes!" he exclaimed, with that how-did-you-know note of surprise, and suddenly all shyness and hesitation disappeared, replaced by pure delight, unrestrained and uninhibited. "It's fantastic!" he said, almost laughing in recollection of this little acrobat that had so recently come into his life.

As he carefully wrote down "white-breasted nuthatch" on his growing list, it was my turn to ask the questions.

"Do you have a field guide?"

He didn't, but he planned to get one "real soon." One more step toward addiction. What would I recommend? There is a baffling choice of field guides now, but my favorite for beginners is still Robbins' *Birds of North America.* I suggested that he buy the paperback edition and keep it handy by the window. I also suggested that he could learn the birds more quickly by going on some of the Audubon Society's field trips with experienced leaders.

He wanted to do that, because he had a lot of woodpeckers that he couldn't sort out and couldn't describe very well. He had an owl, too, that had flown across his yard at dusk. He didn't know what kind it was.

The mention of owls excited my own curiosity, and I asked for his exact location. As he described it, I realized he lived right in the middle of the area assigned to Ted and me for the annual Christmas Bird Count, an area in which we had failed for the past two years to find any owls. Next year he might lead us to one. Next year he might be far enough advanced to participate in the count himself. Already I was planning ahead.

I wrote down his telephone number and asked more questions.

"How far are you from the lake?"

"Oh, just a few blocks," he said, and added that he enjoyed watching the ducks, although he knew little about them. "But I'll tell you my real favorites," he confided. "I love those Canadian geese."

That note was there again, with a touch of awe in it. I didn't tell him that their proper name is Canada geese, not Canadian. He would learn that soon enough. What I did tell him was that one of the memorable experiences of the last Christmas Count was seeing a flock of eight Canada geese come in for a landing on his lake. He had never seen them there, and he accepted this piece of news with outspoken pleasure.

"Isn't that a great sight?" he sighed, and I reflected that people who get hooked on birds are usually hooked first by one bird in particular. With him, it could be the Canada goose—or it could be the amazing little nuthatch.

By that time we were friends, and all evidence of apology faded from his voice as we shared experiences. He wanted to know what other birds he might expect to see on the lake and in his yard. He wanted to know about birdseed, and I was horrified to learn that he was buying ordinary mixed seed and expensive thistle seed and *mixing them together.*

With a real exercise of restraint, I made the gentle suggestion that he was wasting a lot of thistle seed, and that he would actually save money by investing in a special thistle feeder, with small holes into which the finches could thrust their beaks and pick out seeds one by one, without spilling the precious food on the ground—and, I might have added, without wasting it on less desirable visitors.

By the time we said goodbye, he was making plans to visit the Audubon Naturalist Society to buy birdseed, a thistle feeder, and a field guide. He would be needing binoculars, too.

He was well on his way down the endless birding trail. I almost envied him. He had only the faintest glimmer of the world of discovery that lay ahead of him.

He thanked me for my time.

"It's been a pleasure talking to you," I said—and meant it.

"And stop in any time you're out this way," he added.

I planned to do that—before the next Christmas Count. There was that unidentified owl out there . . .

✛

THE OSPREYS ARE BACK

A telephone in the bathroom was never my idea of the ultimate luxury. But there it was, installed by the former owner of our house who must have been summoned, dripping, from the shower one time too many.

We don't really need it and most of the time we forget it's there. But we left it rather than leaving a mar on the wall. It's unobtrusive enough—except when it rings. That harsh jangle, echoing off the walls in that confined space, was undoubtedly designed to overpower the sound of running water, but it has an unsettling effect in an otherwise quiet house.

The first time I heard it at close range I was not in the shower. I was down on my hands and knees laying a spring-green carpet over the coral-pink tiles. It was one of those balmy days when I should have been out birding, but I was concentrating doggedly on the tricky task of fitting the new carpet into odd corners. That awful telephone clamor, close to my ear, broke my concentration and completely unnerved me.

Shaking, I reached for the phone. The voice in my ear was soothing—gentlemanly, refined, and faintly familiar.

"This is Elliott Richardson."

(Ah, yes. I'd heard the voice many times on television, when he was still being addressed as "Mr. Secretary" or "Mr. Attorney General.")

"I hope I'm not calling at an inconvenient time."

"Oh no, not at all," I assured him politely. Happy to be invisible, I settled back on the bathroom floor in the midst of the interrupted project.

He had been fishing at Little Falls that morning, he said, and I recalled reading that he enjoyed fishing as well as birdwatching. Shad were running in the Potomac, and he was having a very good day. To make it perfect, he saw the first ospreys of the season circling over the falls.

There were eight of them, he said, astonished at such numbers. He had never seen so many together.

I had, only once, and it was a sight I would never forget. It was at Cape May, New Jersey, our favorite spot for fall migration. After spending a morning at Cape May Point, watching a steady stream of kestrels and sharp-shinned hawks interspersed with occasional merlins and peregrine falcons, we had gone in the afternoon to Higbee Beach on the Delaware Bay side of the cape. We arrived in time to witness a spectacular flight of ospreys. Following the shoreline, they had just come in, and they were hungry. "Fish hawks," the local people called them, and we watched as the birds went about the serious business of fishing in the bay.

Cruising over the beach, they spotted their targets in the shallow water and hovered for several seconds on powerful wings before descending in a stunning precision dive, talons outstretched to spear the hapless fish. Then, shaking the water from their wings, they flew off to enjoy their meal.

Somewhat back from the beach a large dead tree, barkless and weathered to a smooth silver-gray, provided a picturesque dining area. At one time, we counted 11 ospreys sharing that tree, all unaware of their artistic appearance as they tore into the flesh of the fish held in place with their talons.

It is remarkable how the mere mention of ospreys can reproduce that whole scene for me like an instant replay, in vivid detail. It served as a perfect backdrop without interfering in the least with our conversation.

I didn't tell Elliott Richardson about that scene. It would have been bad form, a crass display of one-upmanship. I simply shared his amazement and delight over his morning's experience.

"I was just wondering," he said, "what they were doing—and why there were so many together."

Actually, they were doing the same thing Mr. Richardson was doing at Little Falls. Ospreys, too, are fond of shad—and, I might add, are far more skillful than humans at dealing with the bones. In the vanguard of the migration, they were hungry, and they recognized a good thing when they saw it. The presence of a fisherman wading out in the water may have inhibited them, but he could be sure they all had a hearty meal after he left. It was probably the abundance of shad at that point that accounted for the number of birds. In any case, it was good news that the ospreys were back—and in such encouraging numbers.

I suspected that Mr. Richardson's main purpose in calling was not to ask questions, but to share that news. It was cause for rejoicing.

We chatted for some time about ospreys—their fishing skills, their elegant combination of power and grace, their alarming decline in the years before we learned of the devastating effects of DDT, their gradual comeback when we righted our wrongs and cleaned up the rivers that were poisoning the fish.

Sitting cross-legged on the bathroom floor, I told Elliott Richardson about the growing number of osprey and eagle nests along Chesapeake Bay, and he expressed the hope, not to be fulfilled for several years, that they would soon be nesting on the Potomac again.

We signed off with the traditional birders' closing: "Good birding!" I returned to my mundane chore, sped on by the renewed awareness that spring was passing me by while I was imprisoned in this small room with only a skylight to give a hint of the outdoor world. But enclosed as I was, that new green carpet had become for a few minutes a magic carpet, transporting me to the banks of the Potomac, to Higbee Beach, and to Chesapeake Bay, as I followed the flight of the ospreys.

COLOR THE THRUSH RED

It is surprising how often complaints come in the guise of questions. Something in the tone of voice gives a clue that the questioner is seeking sympathy, not information.

I heard that wistful tone in the voice of the woman who called with a perfectly natural question: "Are there any places in this area where I can safely go birding by myself?"

She had only recently discovered the world of birds and was eager to be out on the trail every day, making up for lost time. There were not enough guided field trips to satisfy her appetite, so she needed to plan solo adventures.

I made two or three suggestions, but all the while I sensed she had something else on her mind. Was she seeking a birding companion? Or complaining about the shortage of bird-walks led by experts?

Neither.

Just when the conversation seemed to be going nowhere, she came out with it. The crux of the problem was an uncooperative spouse.

"My husband won't go with me," she said, with more than a hint of bitterness. "He says he could never be a birdwatcher because he's colorblind."

Her bitterness was understandable. Her mate's affliction had suddenly became *her* affliction, standing between her and her new-found passion.

She didn't ask me to verify his statement, and I was reluctant to comment on a problem that might better be handled by a marriage counselor. Her husband just might be using this as a convenient excuse to avoid getting involved in an activity that held absolutely no charm for him.

I hesitated, and I was lost.

"Is that true?" she demanded, point-blank.

And so I had to tell her that perfect color vision (if there is such a thing) is not a prerequisite for birdwatching.

I thought at once of my father, who confused shades of brown, gray, red, and green so hopelessly that he was capable of choosing a pair of Kelly-green socks to wear with a sober brown business suit. But when it came to identifying ducks on the wing, he was quick and infallible. And on one of my last visits with him on the farm, when I was struggling, with the aid of binoculars, to identify a bird that was half-concealed by foliage, he looked up and said casually, "Why, that's a cuckoo," as if anyone with normal vision should have known. He was 86 then, and he had never owned a pair of binoculars.

I thought, too, of my son, who is handicapped in the same way and in about the same degree that my father was, for this is a genetic trait passed on from one generation to another, mainly to male offspring through the females. Like his grandfather, Steve has difficulty in distinguishing what he calls "the muddy colors."

But I'm not sure it's correct to call it a handicap. Certainly he doesn't perceive colors the same as his parents do. But we were the ones who were handicapped on a birding trip with him one winter day. He pointed out a hermit thrush, and we couldn't see it at all.

"Right there! Right in front of you," Steve kept saying, but until it moved we were completely frustrated. To us, the thrush's color blended so perfectly with the background of brown leaves that it was virtually invisible, yet to our "color-deficient" son the two shades of brown were sharply distinguishable. For him, the bird might just as well have been flaming red.

I didn't tell my caller about my father or my son, who could best be described as appreciators rather than dedicated birdwatchers. Nor did I think it would be any consolation to her to know how common her mate's deficiency is, affecting eight out of a hundred men, yet only one in 200 women. But I did tell her that one of the keenest birders I know is "colorblind," or "color-deficient," as the vision experts more accurately describe it. They point out that the total absence of color perception, which would reduce the world to images of black, white, and gray, is extremely rare. Less rare is a yellow-blue deficiency. The commonest is the red-green variety, shared by my male relatives.

I was thinking of Hal Wierenga, who falls in the same class— visually if not ornithologically. With 30 years of birding experience, he ranks with the best in the field. His quick eye, his expertise in identification, and his infectious enthusiasm make him a valued birding companion and field-trip guide. Few people who share his trips are aware of his handicap.

"Sure, it's a handicap," he admits readily. "A cardinal against a leafy green background just disappears. And if a cardinal flies in front of the car, everyone sees the red but me. I see only a dark silhouette that could just as well be a thrush."

Hal finds that distance and lighting conditions affect his color perception remarkably. At close range or with binoculars he can distinguish colors that are confusing at a greater distance. And bright sunlight is a hindrance, not a help, tending to wash out the colors. Hal likes nothing better than a dull, gray day in the field.

Here is an acknowledged expert at raptor identification who confesses to problems with the red-tailed hawk. He will observe that the tail is plain, not barred, but he rarely sees it as red. And there are shorebirds that present problems for him because positive identification may depend on subtleties of color that he feels incompetent to judge.

The drab, look-alike Empidonax flycatchers are difficult for him, as they are for most of us. On the other hand, he has no trouble with thrushes in their varying shades of rust, brown, and olive. They have other distinguishing traits, such as behavior (the hermit thrush, for example, has a telltale habit of pumping its tail) and pattern. With most birds, in fact, identification is based not so much on the exact color as on the pattern and *distribution* of color. It is remarkable (and no doubt comforting to the color-deficient) to note the great number of species that are arrayed in black and white and gray, in infinitely varied designs.

I know one color-deficient birder who has specialized in gulls for that specific reason. But not Hal. He enjoys all of them, including the colorful woodland birds.

"I *like* color," he says, "even if I don't see it the same way you do. I enjoy the bright little warblers most of all."

To compensate for his handicap, he relies on other identification clues: songs, call notes, profile, behavior, and habitat. He certainly hasn't let it diminish his enjoyment of birds.

With all this in mind, how should I respond to the birder-convert with a color-deficient spouse?

Common sense dictates: "Don't force the issue." He may not want to pursue birds. Unreasonable as it may seem to us, there are those who find greater happiness on a golf course or a ski slope. But he might be persuaded to spend an afternoon at the zoo, and a stroll past the duck ponds and eagle cages would not be amiss. Beginners, I have observed, like big birds, easy to see, easy to identify, even without benefit of full color vision. A search in the field for small sparrows or even smaller warblers spells frustration. Far more rewarding is a trip to an Eastern Shore refuge at migration time, spring or fall. Few can resist the spell of the migration, when thousands of swans and Canada and snow geese take to the air.

I could make these suggestions and assure her that her husband could find great enjoyment in pursuing birds, if that's what he chose to do. For her sake I hoped he would, not only because it would give her a birding companion but because, when the interest is shared, it can work wonders for a marriage.

But the key is motivation. People have to discover birds for themselves. The vast majority never do.

I have a vivid memory of my color-deficient son, involved in a softball game at a fourth-grade picnic. At a critical point in the game, he stood paralyzed in left field with the ball in his hand while his teammates yelled, "Throw it! Throw it!"

Oblivious, he stood there like a small statue depicting wonder, his mouth slightly open, his eyes wide, gazing at a point across the field.

"Throw it home!" the fans shrieked desperately, and he woke from his trance, seconds too late to make the decisive throw.

What did it matter that his team lost? He scarcely noticed. He was still dazed by the vision of a family of bluebirds flitting through the trees that bordered the playing field. His eyes had caught that electric flash of blue as they flew over the field just at the moment he caught the ball.

He was the only one who saw them.

THERE'S A PTARMIGAN
ON MY WINDOW SILL

It's strange how a single telephone call can upset a well-organized day, disrupting orderly thought processes and changing perspective in such a way that the world seems a little out of focus.

That was the impact of a call from a man I'll call Dr. X, because I don't remember his last name. But I do remember that he identified himself as a doctor, although he was calling on a non-medical matter of mutual interest. He called, he said, at the suggestion of the Audubon Naturalist Society. He had a question to ask, but his question sounded more like a statement.

"I believe I had a ptarmigan on my window sill this morning," he said in a calm, authoritative voice. Then came the question: "Would that be unusual in this part of the country?"

A ptarmigan on a windowsill would be unusual in any part of the country, and in a well-populated suburb of the nation's capital it would be highly unusual, to put it mildly. That was my message, if not my exact wording.

But the doctor was willing to argue his case.

"It had all the appearance of a ptarmigan in spring molt," he said quite reasonably, indicating some knowledge of ptarmigans. "Its head and shoulders were a mottled brown, like a bird coming into summer plumage, and the rest of the body was pure white."

"A ptarmigan is a pretty big bird," I said, trying to picture one in the act of balancing on a windowsill.

"I'm familiar with ptarmigans," he replied. "I was stationed in Iceland for several years. This looked about the size of the ptarmigans I saw there."

I did not want to pit my familiarity with ptarmigans against his. Only twice in my life have I seen ptarmigans, both sightings the result of great patience and persistence.

High in the Rocky Mountains, after days of unrewarding search, Ted and I came upon a small flock of white-tailed ptarmigans browsing on the tundra. It was mid-July, and the protective coloration of their summer plumage was beautifully designed to match the mottled background of mossy rocks and lichens. Eight chicken-sized birds should be easy to see at 15 yards, but if they had not moved we would have passed them by without notice.

On another tundra—a flat, sea-level tundra in northern Manitoba—we saw a pair of willow ptarmigans, again after days of frustrating search and diminishing hopes. It was late June, and the male still wore some of the pure-white winter plumage that is his camouflage against the snow. But his head and the upper part of his body were a mottled chocolate-brown, much as the doctor was now describing to me. But I couldn't imagine that the bird would fit neatly on a windowsill. And since these ptarmigans, members of the grouse family, are rarely seen very far below the Canadian border, I couldn't imagine one of Icelandic origin being as far off-base as Virginia.

The good doctor was not inclined to be pinned down to specifics of size and field marks. He did what many men do when a conversation is going nowhere: He called his wife.

"She's better at describing things than I am," he explained.

She was also more animated. She spoke with a musical lilt in an accent I could not immediately identify. She confirmed her husband's observations, but in doing so she conveyed more than the mere details of the sighting. Her voice revealed delight, excitement, and a certain nostalgia as she added to her description: ". . . just the way our ptarmigans at home looked in the springtime."

"Is it possible?" she faltered, and something in her voice indicated that she already knew it was not.

For a miserable moment I regretted the day I had agreed to be a volunteer bird-identifier. I had not bargained on being the shatterer of wish-fulfillment dreams.

But honesty prevailed. As tactfully as possible, I asked the questions that clearly established the bird for what I knew it must be: an ordinary city pigeon, or rock dove.

Yes, she had noticed that it had pink legs and feet, and it did seem rather small. She had watched it for some time as it walked back and forth on the second-story window sill, making funny little noises unlike any she had heard from a ptarmigan in her native Iceland. It seemed quite tame. It had flown up onto the roof of the house next door. "It might still be there," she said.

Then, to my relief, her initial disappointment turned to surprise, then to genuine pleasure.

She had heard of pigeons; indeed, she had seen a few already. But she thought they were supposed to be a blue-gray color. She was amazed to learn that her oddly mottled visitor in shades of brown and white belonged to the same family.

"But it was so beautiful!" she said. "And is it really common?"

Far from being disappointed that it was not some rarity displaced from its usual habitat, she was eager to be reassured that the bird might live in her neighborhood, might even return to her window sill with a little encouragement.

The next-best thing to encountering an old friend from home, I concluded, was to make a new friend in a new home.

I went back to work with my thoughts turned topsy-turvy as I visualized an ordinary rock dove imbued with rare beauty, and I wondered about those ptarmigans I had pursued so doggedly over the tundra.

The memory that for a time had been so vivid was now as elusive as the ptarmigans themselves had been. Had I really seen them? Or had I, too, been deluded by a wish-fulfillment dream?

THE CARE AND FEEDING OF GULLS

A young man named James Something-or-Other brightened my day with a nine o'clock call from his office in downtown Washington. He was still excited about a white bird he had seen over the parkway as he drove to work. He had just moved up here from the Florida coast, he said, where there were many seagulls. This lone bird looked exactly like them. Could this possibly be a seagull, right here in Washington, D.C.?

Without delivering a lecture on the misnomer "seagull," which is never used by knowledgeable birders, I assured him it was not only possible but quite common to see gulls in Washington, and that if he drove along the Mall he could see a congregation of ring-billed gulls any day of the week.

"So far inland?" he marveled, reflecting a popular misconception that gulls are essentially sea birds. He had never seen flocks of gulls following a tractor in a farm field, nor the screaming gangs that follow garbage trucks on their rounds. The sanitary landfill is the best place I know to study gulls—far better than any of the ocean beaches.

Ring-billed gulls have become city-wise scavengers, feeding on all the edible detritus of our throw-away, fast-food civilization. When James goes to a suburban shopping mall, he will find gulls a-plenty to remind him of his Florida home.

I thought of my kindhearted but misguided friend Nell, who has taken on the personal responsibility of feeding the gulls at a popular shopping mall. Guided by her overprotective instinct and unswerved by factual information, she makes daily visits to the mall with cartons of stale bread, endearing herself to gulls, no doubt, but not to the management, nor to the people who park their cars in this gull heaven.

Nell called me several months ago when she first discovered a few gulls hovering over the mall. "Poor things," she said. "They're starving. There must be a shortage of fish, so they've come all the way from the ocean looking for food."

Like many crusaders, she hears only what she wants to hear. I wasted my breath telling her that these gulls habitually feed inland; that they gather where the food is, and undoubtedly were thriving on popcorn from the theater, half-finished hot dogs from the carry-out, and other scraps dropped casually on the parking lot.

She heard none of it.

"Poor things!" she repeated. And from her next proud report, I learned she was now feeding 250 gulls a day—not to mention a considerable flock of house sparrows and starlings attracted by her largess.

Sometimes I wish I could introduce my callers to one another. James and Nell should get together—and the Cheese Lady from Arlington would make a good third.

I called her the Cheese Lady because I didn't understand her name, which was drowned in a bubble of merry laughter. She was calling to ask about "a flock of big white birds" in her yard. She had never seen them before (although she lived only a stone's throw from the Potomac), and she was laughing hysterically at the flurry of activity in an area where she seldom saw anything but starlings. There were about 30 of these birds, she said, all chasing around like crazy and squabbling among themselves.

It sounded like typical feeding behavior for gulls. But why they should suddenly appear in her back yard was a mystery.

"What are they eating?" I asked curiously.

She burst into another peal of laughter and gasped, "They're eating *che-e-e-ese!*"

She and her husband, she explained, had gone to the senior citizen center where government surplus cheese was being dispensed to all applicants. "Mr. Reagan's che-e-e-ese," she called it, as though the whole thing was a wonderful joke.

Apparently, supply exceeded demand, and they went home with more cheese than they could consume in a year. What to do with it? She initiated a surplus program of her own and began throwing cubes of "Mr. Reagan's cheese" into the back yard—with results too fantastic to believe, too hilarious for words.

Exit the Cheese Lady, laughing. She could teach Nell a thing or two about attracting gulls. And James, with his one lone gull. Wouldn't *he* be delighted by this backyard bonanza?

AS THE CROWS FLY

Crows have few friends in this world. They are so widely reviled and so rarely praised that I have concluded only poets and true naturalists are capable of appreciating them.

The woman who called one day in March may not consider herself a naturalist, but she immediately established herself in my mind as a poet.

Her name was Katherine Scrivener, and she called with this observation: "Every evening at sunset," she said, "a river of crows flows past my house."

A *river of crows*. What an imaginative way to describe that steady stream of birds that passes over while sunset fades and the first stars appear in the darkening sky. How many times I had watched the scene—from a shopping mall or from the car, driving along one of those highways that carry commuters from Washington to their suburban homes in Maryland. How many people must have watched that same scene and wondered, as this poet from Gaithersburg wondered:

"Where are they going?"

"I assume they have been feeding in farm fields," she added, with artless alliteration. "But where are they going at sunset?"

Like the commuters who see them night after night on their homeward trek, the crows are headed for a place of rest after the day's work. Finding strength in numbers and comfort in companionship, they gather in communal roosts of hundreds, sometimes thousands, in groves of trees where they can rest, safe and undisturbed.

The flocks that passed in an endless stream over Gaithersburg would join others from fields and landfills to spend the night at the current rendezvous on Montrose Road in Rockville. For the present they are secure there; but they have grown accustomed to changing their roosts as suburban sprawl has infringed on their bedrooms, trees giving way to parking lots and shopping malls and homes for the hopeful who seek escape from the city.

Crows are adaptable and realistic. They face the facts and adjust. Dispossessed of one roost, they find another. Probably most of the crows on Montrose Road are refugees from the old Gude Nursery, now only a memory. When the chain saws attack their new preserve on Montrose Road, they will move elsewhere. They may travel 30, 40, even 50 miles to seek food; but they will return to the familiar haven at night.

A river of crows. The words conjured an image of a different sort that flashed into my mind on reading a tale of a tragedy witnessed by the ornithologist Alexander Wilson in 1810. He had observed a roost of crows on the flats of an island in the Delaware River, near Newcastle. Since it was "entirely destitute of trees," the adaptable crows roosted among the reeds, "elevated but a little above the high water mark." Caught just as humans sometimes are in a sudden, severe storm with rapidly rising waters, crows in great numbers were drowned when their entire roost was submerged.

"Thousands of them were next day seen floating in the river," Wilson wrote, "and the wind shifting to the northwest drove their dead bodies to the Jersey side, where for miles they blackened the whole shore."

That ghastly vision of quite a different "river of crows" returned to haunt me as I talked to Katherine Scrivener. She thanked me for resolving the mystery that had nagged at her for some time and closed the conversation most graciously: "I hope something lovely happens to *you* today."

I knew then that this daily scene of crows floating by in silhouette against the sunset sky was to her a thing of beauty to anticipate and to cherish. This set her apart from the mainstream of public opinion, which holds crows in low regard.

For all their services to mankind, crows get precious little gratitude. Instead they are cast as villains, shot by self-righteous gunmen who see them as a menace to crops besides being an ugly blight on the landscape.

"Corn thieves," the Midwest farmers used to call them, unaware that the crows probably did more good than harm. The corn they gleaned in the fall was only reasonable compensation for all the crop-threatening grubs and insects they consumed throughout the year.

So the farmers put up scarecrows and residents of neat suburban homes try other means to discourage crows. No one wants them as neighbors. "Noisy things!" a friend complained, casting a suspicious eye on a pair that showed signs of nesting in a tree adjacent to her house. She had had crow neighbors before and was not eager to repeat the experience.

There are worse complaints. Crows harass hawks and owls. They steal the eggs, sometimes even the young, from the nests of smaller, more lovable birds. Consequently, they are under attack as often as they are on the attack. It is a familiar sight in the nesting season to see a pair of red-winged blackbirds in relentless pursuit of a lone crow that has loitered too near their nest. Sometimes, if you watch closely, you may see the crow drop the egg it has snatched from the nest. More often it is beaten off and frustrated in its attempted theft.

But crows are tenacious and not easily outwitted. Veteran crow-watchers credit them with a high order of intelligence and a remarkable aptitude for problem-solving. There is probably an element of truth to the familiar fable about the clever crow who dropped pebbles into a pitcher to raise the water level high enough so that he could drink from it. Crows have been known to untie knots and even to extract crackers from those tightly-sealed plastic packages that frustrate and exasperate most humans.

My friend, Lloyd Luther, once watched a street-smart crow struggling to make off with two half-slices of bread found in a gutter. Time and again, the bird attempted to get the slices into its beak and fly off with them, only to lose one or both slices and have to start over. Finally, after a pause to analyze the situation seriously, the wise bird stacked one slice on top of the other, took the "sandwich" in its beak, and flew away, triumphant.

We can thank the omnivorous crows for cleaning up the carcasses of dead animals that litter our highways, and we ought to admire them for their agility in escaping slaughter on the highways themselves. As many times as I have seen crows gathered together to feast on a road kill, I have never yet struck a crow nor seen one struck by another car. They keep a wary watch on traffic and always fly up, just in time.

Nor have I ever seen crows quarreling over food along the road or in the fields. They share naturally and peaceably, unlike the screaming, bickering starlings, which seem to fight over every morsel.

As community-minded as they are, it seems strange that crows forsake their sociable way of life during the nesting season. Before long, those great flocks that have shared a roost throughout the winter months will disperse and go their separate ways to build nests and raise their young.

"Not in *my* back yard, I hope," says my friend. "Noisy things!"

I wonder whether Katherine Scrivener would welcome them as neighbors there in Gaithersburg, whether she would find as much to admire in the individual bird as in the aggregation. I like to think she would rejoice in the sight of fledgling crows, noisy as they are. Surely she would welcome the newcomers, knowing as she does that it takes many crows to make a river.

THE CASE OF THE UNHOODED WARBLER

One of the most treasured rituals of spring is checking off the warblers as they come through in migration: blue-wings, golden-wings, bay-breasted, chestnut-sided . . . all those beautiful little birds with their intriguing names. In a good year we can hope to see 30 different species here, if only fleetingly.

This, however, was not a good year. By mid-May there were significant gaps in our list, in spite of a prime-time visit to Pt. Pelee, the famed birding hotspot in southern Ontario where weary migrants drop down to rest after the strenuous flight across Lake Erie.

This year, it seemed, there were more birders than birds. It was not like the good old days, I reflected, as I settled back into the routine of household chores at the end of the trip. On our first visit to Pt. Pelee we had counted 19 species of warblers in the first half-hour—many of them in great numbers, most of them at close range, low in the bushes or on the ground.

I remembered a Canada warbler that kept us company for several minutes on the woodland path, staying only a few feet ahead of us. And a magnificent hooded warbler that posed on a decayed stump, then hopped down into a shaft of sunlight that illuminated his fresh gold plumage, and the black velvet of his throat and hood.

This year we saw neither the Canada nor the hooded. There had been a wave of orioles at Pt. Pelee, both orchard and northern, chasing through the woods and singing constantly. But warblers were scarce.

Mulling over the mystery of the migration as I put lunch on the table, I heard the ring of the telephone.

"Bird call!" Ted announced, and I picked it up to confront

another mystery.

The caller, who identified herself simply as Delia, was puzzling over a strange warbler she had seen in Virginia, on the Mt. Vernon Parkway. Like all good birders, she was eager to have the mystery solved for her own peace of mind, but it was doubly important because she was participating in a spring birdathon, in which every species identified counts toward a prize.

The bird was mostly yellow, she said, and she thought at first that it was a hooded warbler because she saw the bold black patch on its throat. But the patch stopped there. There was no black on its head! How could that be?

We discussed the possibilities, ruling out one after another. It couldn't be a golden-wing because it had a yellow breast, and it couldn't be the hybrid Lawrence's warbler because it had no black eye-patch.

"I *think* I saw wing-bars," she said, "but I'm not sure. I've looked all through the book and, to tell the truth, the closest thing to it is the Bachman's warbler."

She said this very tentatively, and for good reason. Discovering a Bachman's warbler is the ultimate birder's fantasy. A southern warbler, it is described in the field guides as "rare and endangered, possibly extinct."

Whatever Delia had seen on the Mt. Vernon Parkway, it was surely not a Bachman's warbler. Any thought of such phenomenal luck was quickly dispelled when she added, "It was singing a most beautiful song. And I heard more of them along the parkway—maybe half a dozen."

I have never heard a Bachman's warbler and have no hope that I ever will. But I have listened to the buzzy, unmusical song on tapes. It could hardly be described as beautiful. And half-a-dozen Bachman's? Only in a dream.

Lunch was on the table.

"Let me think about it and call you back," I said. Delia's mystery warbler became the prime topic of our lunch-time conversation.

It simply couldn't be a warbler, we concluded, after reviewing the possible candidates. Scrap the whole idea of a warbler and consider the question, "What yellow bird with a black throat (and possibly wing-bars) sings a beautiful song?"

The answer came instantaneously, with a flash of memory from the scene at Pt. Pelee, where orchard and northern orioles had been flitting through the woods. Among them was a first-year male orchard oriole, singing just as beautifully as his elders, but wearing entirely different plumage. Who would guess on first sight that this dull-yellow bird with the black throat was related to the richly-hued, burnt orange and black adult male?

I recalled with amusement a story told by our friend Bob Hahn, a seasoned birder who won the awe and admiration of a pair of beginners who asked his help in identifying this baffling bird.

When he said, quite casually, "That's a first-year male orchard oriole," they viewed him as an ornithological genius.

"You mean," said one of them, "you can actually tell a bird's *age* just by looking at it?"

I shared that story with Delia when I called her back to suggest that she look at the picture in her field guide on page 302.

"That's it!" she exclaimed, and in the background I could hear her husband echo, "That's it! I *told* you I saw wing-bars."

They were a trifle chagrined at mistaking an oriole for a small warbler. But as I pointed out, the orchard oriole is the smallest of the family, and size is the field-mark most frequently misjudged.

It was easy to believe that they had heard a half-dozen orchard orioles singing along the parkway on a May morning. It just happened that the only one they actually saw as he sang was the young male with the yellow breast and black throat.

The mystery solved, Delia sighed with relief. "Now I can go to sleep tonight."

And so could I—remembering the delightful song of the orchard oriole.

✥

IN A DIFFERENT LIGHT

Bird descriptions by amateurs can tax the imagination. After several puzzling calls about "all those white birds that are flying over," I consulted with Phil DuMont, one of the senior members of the original bird-identifier team, who is especially gifted in guessing how a novice is likely to misperceive a common bird.

"They can't be gulls," I told him. "They're too small. About robin-sized, one man said. And they have long tails."

Phil chuckled. "Those are blue jays migrating over," he said. "People who don't know blue jays think of them as white birds when they see them from underneath."

Another mystery solved. Unfortunately, Phil was not here when I was faced with the pink-bird puzzle, so I had to use my own imagination. It was a case of "I'll have to call you back," giving me time to mull it over. Reviewing my notes at odd moments during the day, I tried to remember exactly what the woman had said.

"What are those big pink birds I see flying over every evening?"

"Flying over where?" I asked. She could have been calling from Florida, which is not unheard of these days, in which case flamingos or spoonbills would be reasonable guesses.

As it turned out she was calling from less than a mile away, and the birds had been seen right over her house.

Flamingos over Bethesda, Maryland? Not likely.

"They're *big* birds," she elaborated, "and all pink, except for a little black at the ends of the wings."

"How many have you seen?" I asked.

"Oh, they come in flocks of a dozen or more, and they fly in formation, sort of. Could they be hawks?"

After assuring her that we don't have pink hawks, I suggested that I call her back after giving the matter some thought.

When the answer came to me, it was so obvious that I was embarrassed.

I had worked in the garden until sunset and, looking up at the rosy sky, I realized it was time to start dinner. A flock of ring-billed gulls flew over on their nightly route from the county landfill to the Mall in Washington, where they gather at day's end. They were followed by another group of a dozen or so—graceful white birds with black-tipped wings, flying in a loose V-formation. In a couple of minutes they would fly right over the home of the lady who had seen the "big pink birds" flying over every evening.

I called her.

"Have you seen your pink birds this evening?"

"I'm looking at them right now from my kitchen window."

And of course she was surprised to learn that they were really pure-white birds, stained a lovely pink by the warm glow of sunset.

Experienced observers make allowances for lighting conditions. They have learned that the ruby throat of a hummingbird, seen in the shade, will appear black, completely lacking the gem-like glitter produced by sunlight. And they are not likely to be fooled by the appearance of a crow with white wing patches, knowing from past observations that those patches are merely the reflections of light on the glossy black wings.

Contemplating the effect of light on color perception, I recalled our first expedition to southeast Arizona, when we were still in the beginner class. We were lucky enough to have the guidance of a trio of hospitable local birders and jumped at their generous offer to take us to a remote canyon to find the rare buff-breasted flycatcher, a bird we hadn't even hoped to add to our life-list on that trip.

After a horrendous, jolting journey up a steep, rocky road that we easterners would have considered impassable, we arrived, dusty and perspiring, at the head of the canyon. A grove of cottonwoods, shimmering in the noonday sun, cast their shade over a small stream. The trickle of water over rocks was the only sound in the breathless air. The place seemed barren of all life except our own. We had, it appeared, made this monumental effort for nothing.

Disheartened, we unpacked lunches and thermoses.

Our leader *pro tem* suddenly froze in listening attitude.

"That's it!" he whispered.

There was a soft "quit, quit" from high in the branches. Shielding my eyes from the glare, I looked up, my heart beating suffocatingly from the heat—or from the excitement of being in the presence of a life-bird.

Three small birds were darting out from perches to capture flying insects, three elusive buff-breasted flycatchers. My binoculars moved from one to the other. It was hardly a great aesthetic experience. I wasn't at all sure that these pale specimens were worth the trip. This could be any insignificant little Empidonax.

Ted's reaction was the same. We looked at each other in unspoken dismay: *These* are buff-breasted flycatchers?

It was not until we were finishing our lunch under the protective trees that we got the life-bird view we expected. The flycatchers, by that time accustomed to our presence, had moved down to the lower branches and were making quick forays out over the stream. Seen in the shade, unbleached by the dazzling sun, they were lovely little birds, their rich, tawny hue deserving of their name. Only then did we feel entitled to add them to our life-list.

But far more important than adding a species to our life-list, we had learned something about lighting and color. The lesson promised to make us better birders.

THE MISSISSIPPI
WOOD DUCK MURDERS

A call from my brother Phil usually turns out to be a bird call. No matter what the initial topic is, sooner or later we get around to birds.

Phil lives in the Illinois town of Nauvoo, where I was born, a scenic spot on the Mississippi River. From that vantage point he keeps a watch on the comings and goings of birds along the Mississippi Flyway.

In fall he reports on the arrival of ducks and Canada geese. In winter he reports on the numbers of bald eagles he sees feeding on fish in the shallow waters below the dam at Keokuk, Iowa. Now and then he sights an unusual bird or observes unusual bird behavior that he likes to share with me.

When he called one day in May to talk specifically about wood ducks, I had an instant flashback of a scene he had shown me on my last visit to Nauvoo.

He had taken me for a drive over the scenic highway that follows the river south to Hamilton. The Mississippi is wide here, and the highway affords splendid views of the blue-green bluffs on the Iowa side. We parked at a bend in the river where there is a broad expanse of marsh along the shore with a luxurious growth of water lilies.

When my eyes became accustomed to the shimmering light on the lily pads, I saw what he had taken me there to see. The marsh was alive with wood ducks, floating inconspicuously about among the masses of vegetation.

I had never seen so many together. The males, with their glistening red eyes and hand-painted coloring, were easier to spot than the modest gray females with their camouflage spots. There must have been 30 or more, drifting in and out of sight among the lilies.

This was a sanctuary now, Phil told me, and he pointed out the housing project that, along with favorable feeding conditions, had attracted so many wood ducks. Man-made nesting boxes had been erected on metal poles at intervals in the marsh, and these dwellings had proved highly satisfactory to the tenants as an alternative to their customary homes in tree cavities.

It was such a peaceful scene: ducks and water lilies against a backdrop of smooth river and hazy, distant bluffs. Now, with the mere mention of wood ducks, I recalled not only the visual image but the feeling of serenity it produced.

But all was not serene in the wood duck community. That was Phil's message. He told a story of mayhem and murder in that quiet sanctuary.

It was sad. The project had been going so well. The duck population had been increasing steadily each year since the nesting boxes were put in place: from 40 pairs to 60, then 73, according to counts conducted by the Illinois Department of Conservation, which monitored the project.

Then they began to find battered females on the nests. Shy, peaceable lady wood ducks sitting on clutches of eggs showed signs of physical abuse. Several bore identical head wounds and patches of bare skin around the eyes where feathers had been plucked out. All appeared to have been victims of the same attacker. But what manner of predator would inflict such damage?

The grim story became grimmer. When dead bodies were found on nests, the biologists who monitored the project stepped up their vigil. The mystery was solved when they opened a box and surprised the culprit in the act.

It was another female wood duck.

Apparently the project had succeeded all too well, resulting in overcrowding that in turn produced keen competition—deadly competition. Female wood ducks were literally committing murder for possession of scarce housing.

Phil, somewhat shocked by the revelation, asked if I had ever heard of such a story. I had not. I was shocked, too, remembering that peaceful scene on the Mississippi. I would not have thought it possible.

I *did* know that female wood ducks sometimes parasitized other wood duck nests, resorting to a practice known as "dumping." A female unable to find a nesting cavity of her own in a hollow tree or log would "dump" her clutch of eggs in an already established nest, much in the manner of the female cowbird. But unlike the cowbird, she would not go on her merry way; she might actually do battle with the other female over the privilege of brooding both clutches. No matter who won, the result was an over-large brood—and a number of unhatched eggs because the brooding female was unable to cover them all.

This, too, was happening at the Nauvoo sanctuary, Phil said. Nests had been found with as many as 40 eggs, and inevitably about half of them were wasted. Strife between the females continued even after hatching, when the two mothers would have a custody fight over the mixed brood.

Living in the wild without human intervention, wood ducks disperse and seek out nesting sites with enough surrounding acreage to allow them breathing space. Here in this crowded sanctuary, they were adjusting—badly—to unnatural conditions.

It gave us both something to ponder. Man's best intentions sometimes go astray. The planners who set out to create a haven for wood ducks on the Mississippi found that they had created an avian bedlam.

shafer

✥

SLOW DAYS OF SUMMER

The frenetic pace of the migration is over. The last blackpoll is on its way north. The year-round residents who nested earlier are already feeding a new generation of chickadees, titmice, and cardinals. Some have settled down to start on a second brood; their voices are seldom heard. Summer residents, having established their territories and won their mates, have little motivation to sing. They are preoccupied with building or brooding.

It has all happened once more just as it was supposed to happen. Tensions relax. A pervasive quiet descends over us, like a sigh of relief.

But the telephone still rings . . .

CLOSELY WATCHED FINCHES

House finches have become as common as house sparrows in these parts. Here on Melody Lane, in fact, they have effectively displaced the sparrows.

Not that I mind. The finches are more colorful and far more melodious. In general, they make pleasant neighbors. But like the sparrows, they multiply at a scandalous rate, and they make off with costly quantities of sunflower seed.

I can remember when house finches were rarities in the East. Birdwatchers puzzled over them, usually mistaking them for the purple finches that are often here in winter. The original Peterson *Field Guide to the Birds*, which was subtitled "Giving Field Marks of All Species Found East of the Rockies," didn't even mention them. They were western birds.

They came to the East as illegal aliens, shipped from California by crafty dealers who sold them to Long Island pet stores as "Hollywood finches." Buyers, on discovering that these were not legitimate cage birds, released them rather than risk being caught violating the Migratory Bird Treaty Act.

That was in 1940. Thirty years later I saw my first house finch in Cape May, New Jersey. By that time, these accidental immigrants had established themselves up and down the coast, from New England to the Carolinas. Sixteen years ago we fed our first house finch in our Maryland back yard. Now we feed as many as 30. Six pairs nest on our grounds; others join them each day at the sunflower feeder.

"Spreading," notes the revised Peterson *Field Guide to Birds East of the Rockies*. "Exploding," say birders, who have begun to classify them as "trash birds" because of their abundance in city, suburb, and farmland.

But surprisingly, they are strangers to most local residents. I calculate that 90 percent of my bird identification calls are about house finches.

A secretary at the World Bank, only a few blocks from the White House, called one fine June day, marveling at the pretty little birds singing a joyful chorus just outside her office heedless of the city traffic passing by. A celebrity in the crowd could not have excited her half as much as this discovery. What were those little brown birds with the bright red breasts and red top-knots?

I knew what they were before she described them. No other species appears in such numbers along our city streets, except for the unmusical pigeons and starlings. Quite at home in these surroundings, the house finches sing their bubbly song for anyone who will listen, and they continue to sing throughout the summer, when many other songbirds are quiet.

I first heard that song from a hotel window in San Francisco, long before the house finch was established in the East. To my prejudiced ear it was not as pretty as the music of the purple finches passing through our area in spring migration. Nor were the birds themselves as pretty, I thought. They wore a duller shade of red than the bright, clear raspberry hue of the "purple" finch.

This natural preference may have something to do with relative abundance. I suppose if starlings were rare, we would find them more attractive. I can't say that house finches are unwelcome on our property now, as starlings certainly are, but in the winter when they gather around the feeder I scarcely notice them except to search the flocks occasionally for a chance purple finch in their midst. And purple finches, it seems, used to visit us more often and in greater numbers in winters past. Some say the house finches have scared them away—another black mark for the newcomers.

But if veteran birders bear a grudge against the intruders, there are city dwellers who take great delight in them. I know this from the number of telephone calls I've received on the subject.

There was a housewife on the sixth floor of a condominium

who found a pair nesting in a hanging basket on her balcony—a basket that also held a cherished plant. She was full of questions. What were these birds, and how did they happen to nest at that elevation?

She was also full of concern—for the birds and their progeny and for her fuchsia. How could she water it without disturbing them? What should she feed them? And how would the baby birds learn to fly from such a height without injuring themselves?

I set her mind at rest, I think, assuring her that since the finches had chosen to share her balcony, they were unlikely to be disturbed by her presence when she watered the plants. And I suggested that she let the parents worry about flight instruction when the time came. They would not take their responsibility lightly.

Another apartment dweller in the heart of the city had a different problem with the house finches on her balcony. She knew what they were, and she took pleasure in feeding them. But her offerings also attracted a flock of city pigeons that perched on her balcony railing, to the considerable distaste of the neighbors—especially those who liked to sit on the balcony below hers.

How could she discourage the pigeons without starving her adopted finches? This was a matter of importance to her. She was willing to go to some trouble to solve the problem. My suggestion delighted her and prompted her to set off at once to the nearest hardware store.

The idea was simple enough: Enclose the feeder in a wire cage with mesh large enough to permit finches to enter but small enough to keep pigeons out. She lost no time in executing the plan and called later to let me know it had worked perfectly.

Not all endings are so happy. I still feel a twinge when I recall my first conversation with Mrs. Callen, a lady with a gentle, musical voice. She, too, lived in the city and fed the finches. She called them purple finches, but it was long past migration time, so I knew she was feeding resident house finches. I didn't correct her because it didn't seem important, and she hadn't asked for identification help. In fact, she didn't really ask for anything.

Apparently she just wanted to tell me about "her" finches. She was pleased to note that their numbers were increasing steadily. She commented on their lovely chorus, on their behavior at the feeder, and on the variations in their coloring. The males, she said, came in many shades of red, some she described as "Chinese red," almost orange. But she thought the plain little grayish females were pretty, too, in their quiet way.

I decided that Mrs. Callen just wanted to talk about birds, and that was all right with me. We had a pleasant chat and she said, just a trifle apologetically, "I hope you don't mind if I call you sometimes. I enjoy my birds so much, and it's just nice to share them with someone who feels the same way I do."

Of course I didn't mind. Birds are meant to be shared.

"I haven't always paid so much attention to birds," she went on, voicing a regret that many of us feel when we recognize past blindness. "But now I know how they can brighten a day. I don't get out much—my husband is an invalid—so I have more time now to watch the birds from my window."

That's when I said the wrong thing.

"I hope your husband enjoys them, too," I said, thinking of how much comfort an invalid can find in the world of nature.

"No," she said, in that gentle voice that carried both dignity and sadness and without a trace of self-pity. "I'm afraid he's past that."

And so she calls me now and then to talk about the finches that are as common as house sparrows in the city. After we've talked, I always take a closer look at the lovely finches I so often take for granted.

NESTS, LOST AND FOUND

The cheery babble of the resident house wren announced that all was well on that clear summer morning. But I awoke with a vague sense of loss. Something was missing, and to make matters worse, I couldn't remember what it was.

An early telephone call jogged my memory and saved my sanity. The subject was nests, as it often is these days. As it turned out, it was yet another caller who had discovered house finches nesting alongside a plant in a hanging basket on his porch and was wondering whether he could safely water the plant without disturbing the birds.

This touching concern for the preservation of life brought back my own nagging concern. I had lost a nest. In the space of 24 hours, I had found and lost a nest with a yellow-throated vireo sitting on it.

I had found it quite by accident after a visit to the nest of bald eagles on an island in the Potomac, within easy viewing distance of the shore and, fortunately, within easy commuting distance from home. I felt a proprietary interest in that nest, having watched the eagles build it, so I made regular pilgrimages to the lookout point, where I gazed through the spotting scope at the satisfying sight of the female sitting on the nest, the male standing guard nearby.

A nest is a symbol of hope. The hopes of many watchers were centered on that eagle nest, the first to appear along the Potomac in 30 years, and there was great anxiety over the daring pair so exposed to public view. It was a day of relief and rejoicing when the scope revealed two floppy, fuzzy chicks being fed by the attentive parents.

Few people have the privilege of watching young eaglets on a nest, and I took full advantage as they grew and shed their fuzz for real feathers. When they began to flap their wings, I began to make daily trips to the overlook, hoping to be there at the magic moment of flight.

It was on one of those trips, when half a dozen eager spectators were watching the eaglets languishing in the nest with no sign of imminent takeoff, that I discovered the other nest and its quiet occupant.

The male vireo inadvertently called attention to it, fluttering about and landing on a low limb within arm's reach of the path as I walked by. Stopping to admire him, I glanced beyond him and saw his mate seated on her tidy hanging nest in a tangle of honeysuckle vines, only a few feet away from me and just slightly above eye level.

It seemed such a public place for a small bird to be nesting, with hikers and joggers and strollers passing by at all hours, not to mention the growing numbers of eagle-watchers. But I consoled myself with the thought that most of the passersby had other things on their minds; most, in fact, were not even aware of the massive eagle nest on the island, so they would surely overlook anything as small as a vireo's nest, which was, after all, cleverly camouflaged. Maybe no one else would ever find it, although to me it was so obvious. Maybe I would have the exclusive privilege of watching the vireo nest.

I remembered exactly where it was. Or I thought I did. But on the next day's visit, after finding the eaglets still clinging to their home base, I searched in vain for the little hanging nest. Tracing and retracing my route, up and down the towpath I walked, peering into countless tangles of honeysuckle and finding— nothing.

It was a mystery. How could a nest disappear overnight? An abandoned nest I could understand, but to find no nest at all was inconceivable. At last I was forced to give up.

After the house finch call was settled, I determined to go back and give it another try. But I was delayed by another call, this one from a woman who wanted help in identifying a bird that had her terribly worried. The bird, she reported in some distress, had a nest *on the ground!*

She was apparently under the impression that all sensible birds nest in trees, and for good reason, too. Her husband had nearly run over this nest with his mower, but the bird had flown up and distracted him by pretending it was injured.

He had found the nest, which was not much more than a hollowed-out place on the ground, with four splotchy greenish eggs in it. For a couple of weeks he had carefully mowed around it, hoping that these birds knew what they were doing. Three of the eggs had hatched; the fourth was inactive. But there were those three little babies *on the ground*, and what should they do about it?

Again, this touching concern for the preservation of life.

She had already told me enough to identify the bird as a killdeer.

"A *what?*" she asked, as if I had spoken to her in Greek.

"Killdeer," I repeated. "They're named for the call they give. It sounds like 'Kill-deer, kill-deer!'"

She recognized the call from my poor imitation, for she had heard it many times, especially when the startled bird flew up "like a flash of silver—beautiful!" Actually, the killdeer is not silver, but may appear so when seen in flight because of its white underparts. On the ground, it shows a warm beige back, two distinctive black bands around its neck and, when it spreads its tail, a splash of orange.

The woman had seen that outspread tail when the killdeer went into its "distraction display" to lure humans away from the young birds, and she described quite accurately the way the parent pretended to be injured, just to divert attention. She was amazed to know that this "broken-wing act" is typical of killdeer, and even more amazed to learn that these birds always nest on the ground, depending on their wits to protect both nest and offspring.

Having assured her that there was nothing she needed to do to rescue the young killdeer family, I returned to the nagging mystery of the vireo nest. I couldn't wait to resume the search. The eaglets had taken second place to this obsession.

Hurrying to finish interrupted household chores, I went out to water the plants on the screened porch. My eyes suddenly rested on a dark clump in the andromeda bush just beyond the screen. It looked like a nest.

It *was* a nest. Against the greenery, I could make out the silhouette of a cardinal sitting on it.

How long had it been there? How many times had I stood in this same spot without seeing it? It was so inconspicuous and its occupant was so quiet that even our indoor cats, who spend much time on the porch, had never given a sign of noticing it.

There is something infinitely relaxing about watching a bird brooding on a nest. I poured a cup of coffee and settled down in a quiet corner of the porch. Ten feet away, the patient cardinal sat without moving. Ten feet beyond her, baby wrens were clamoring in their nesting box, while in the background the bubbling song of the parent wren gave repeated assurances that all was well.

Content, I lost the urgent need to dash out on another fruitless search. If I could overlook this cardinal's nest, I could overlook a vireo's nest, even when I knew so well where it was. I had to trust the vireos to know what they were doing and to hatch their brood without my supervision.

I could go out later to check up on the eagles. For the moment, it was enough to keep a close watch on my quiet cardinal.

A MOST PECULIAR BIRD

Bill Yates had a strange bird in his yard. He had puzzled over it for a long time before he called me.

"I've never seen anything like it," he said. "It's the most peculiar bird I've ever seen."

That's what people usually say about birds they can't identify. As often as not, the peculiar bird turns out to be a something as commonplace as a house finch.

Indeed, that was my first guess about Mr. Yates' bird. He said it had a nest in a broken drainpipe under the eaves, and that's the kind of place a house finch might choose for a nest.

Luckily, I kept my guess to myself. The bird that Mr. Yates went on to describe in careful detail was certainly not a house finch. There was actually a pair of them, he said, and he had been watching them ever since the days of their courtship. He had continued to watch them, at fairly close range and with binoculars, during the nest-building phase. Now the female was sitting on the nest while her mate came and went, and he still hadn't the foggiest idea what they were. He could find nothing in his bird book that fit the picture.

The female he wrote off as "just a nondescript sparrow-like bird, brownish above and dingy-beige below," with no distinctive markings. But the male was something else, quite a handsome fellow. He had a brown back and wings, with a white wing-stripe. But his head was a remarkable combination of slate-gray, rusty brown, black, and white.

It did sound colorful, and I searched my memory for a bird that sported such a combination. I stopped puzzling when Mr. Yates described how these colors were distributed: slate-gray on the crown and cheek, a broad stripe of rust through the eye, a patch of white along the neck, and black around the beak, extending down over the throat like a bib.

I listened to the amazingly precise recital, probably read from Mr. Yates' notes, and the mental picture came out sharp and clear.

Never had I heard a house sparrow described in such minute detail.

But when I gave Mr. Yates my diagnosis, he didn't seem to hear me. He went on to discuss their vocalization. He had heard them uttering "cheep" notes, and he thought he had heard the male singing "a more elaborate tune," but he did not trust his failing hearing. The song might have been that of another bird.

I tried to return to the house sparrow idea, but he ignored the suggestion as if unworthy of comment.

"I've taken some pictures," he said, "and I hope they turn out. May I send them to you so that you can have a look for yourself?"

Before the pictures arrived Mr. Yates called again, in some excitement.

"Would you believe it? I have a whole *flock* of those birds in my yard now!"

I did believe it. As summer advanced, I was seeing flocks of house sparrows gathering on lawns to feed. But Mr. Yates remained deaf to my opinions. His pictures had come back and they looked "pretty fair." He would send me a few of them.

The pictures arrived with a note: "I enclose nine photos of the mysterious bird and his mate. If you can identify him I would be most pleased. His colors changed as the mating season progressed. The slate color on top of his head and the black on his breast turned darker."

While I was still trying to phrase a diplomatic response to Mr. Yates, standing by my initial identification, he called and saved me the trouble.

"I've figured out that mystery bird!" he announced triumphantly. "It's a house sparrow!"

Well, imagine that.

Then he explained how he had missed it in the first place. He had looked at all the sparrows in the book and it didn't match any of them.

"But a house sparrow isn't really a sparrow," he explained. "It's a weaver finch, and it's in another part of the book."

So it is. I should have told him that in the first place. It might have saved us a lot of time.

But it's a lot more satisfying to solve your own mysteries. I think Bill Yates would agree. And long summer days are ideal for pondering mysteries—and studying house sparrows. It's a game anyone can play.

✤

TROUBLESOME BIRDS
ARE ALL MY FAULT

Among the minor injustices in this unjust world is the blame heaped upon us Audubon types whenever a bird misbehaves or causes distress.

I have been held personally responsible for mockingbirds that keep people awake at night, for woodpeckers that inflict damage on dwellings, for chickadees that take over nesting boxes intended for bluebirds, and starlings (for whom I make no excuses) that mess up freshly-bathed cars.

When I hear an accusatory voice on the telephone, I steel myself for the announcement that one of "my" birds has done wrong.

"One of your little darlings," began an uncommonly aggrieved voice, "is going to get its neck wrung if I ever catch it."

The offender turned out to be not an odious starling or house sparrow or a messy grackle, but a friendly robin.

"He sits all day on my car and defecates," the plaintiff deposed. "Always *my* car. With all the other cars on the block, he searches out *my* car. I move it around and he always finds it. It doesn't matter whether I park it on the street or on the carport. He comes right up onto the carport, and if there are two cars side by side, he goes straight to *my* car and parks on it."

"And what does he do?" I prompted, searching for a reasonable avian motive.

"He defecates," she replied promptly.

I hesitated to suggest that this could scarcely be a full-time activity, or even the robin's major purpose in seeking out her car.

"What else does he do?" I persisted.

She thought for a moment. "He walks up to the windshield and stares at it."

Ah, a clue!

"Maybe he sees his reflection there and is confused. He may think it's a rival robin."

"Why does it have to be *my* windshield?" she complained. "There are plenty of other windshields around."

I felt impelled to protect the robin's reputation. The lady was clearly viewing this as an act of sheer malice directed at her personally, and I wanted to assure her, from my long acquaintance with robins, that malice is not in their makeup. But I could only speculate on the bird's mental processes.

"If he first saw the reflection in your windshield, it might not occur to him that he could find it anyplace else."

She was not inclined to be charitable. After muttering something that sounded like "bird-brain," she demanded, "How do I get rid of him? I'm not going to spend my life washing the car."

The solution seemed simple to me: Cover the windshield with a towel. But that was too much bother—almost as much bother as washing the car. Surely I could suggest an easier way to discourage a demented robin.

Under pressure for an acceptable answer, I recalled the experience of a man who was having problems with swallows roosting in his boathouse, to the detriment of a new paint job on his boat. He placed a plastic owl in a prominent place on the boat and the offending swallows fled immediately.

I offered this idea as a last resort to the robin-plagued lady, convinced before I spoke that this, too, would be too much bother for her. To my surprise, she grasped it with real enthusiasm.

"Now that's a good idea. My husband is an artist. I'll get him to make me a papier-mache owl. He'll enjoy doing something useful."

I had the feeling that the motives of artists and robins were beyond her comprehension, but I was relieved to have won a stay of execution for the robin.

"Let me know if it works," I said.

"I'll let you know if it *doesn't*," she retorted, with an implied threat that could not be ignored. Clearly, the bird was my responsibility.

She hasn't called again. But my line has been busy with other bird problems. There's this nutty cardinal pecking on a window all day, and an overly aggressive mockingbird that chases all the good little birds away, and a pack of ravenous house finches that are driving a bird-feeding benefactor into bankruptcy.

And what, my callers ask, am I going to do about them?

HERE COMES THE BRIDE!

"It was a lovely wedding," the lady told me. She thought I would be especially pleased to know that no rice was thrown at the happy couple as they left the church.

Good common sense, I agreed. Why waste the rice? And it does present a slippery hazard underfoot on the church steps.

"Instead of rice," my informant continued, "they gave all the guests little bags of birdseed. Isn't that a great idea?"

It's a great idea for those who sell birdseed. Through clever packaging, they can increase their profit 200 percent. Never mind that the birds have plenty of natural food available in June, the traditional month for weddings. There are always opportunistic house sparrows and starlings ready to take advantage of a good thing.

But I was missing her point. Her point was that people have become wise to the fact that innocent birds are being killed by eating rice tossed about on church premises. She was sure I knew this, but she was afraid that many of my readers did not, so she hoped I would spread the word in my column.

What she was repeating in good faith and with all good intentions was a myth that has been around for a number of years, one that keeps cropping up in print from time to time although it has been discredited by all authorities. In the old days when great flocks of bobolinks used to descend on the rice fields in the South, farmers may well have wished that these poachers would drop dead. But the only risk to the bobolinks, commonly known as "rice birds," came from irate farmers who shot them by the thousands to protect their crops.

"There is absolutely no truth to the belief that rice can kill birds," says Steven C. Sibley of the Cornell Laboratory of Ornithology.

Nevertheless, the myth persists, in contradiction of all scientific evidence. Like most myths, its origins are lost in history. But it gained publicity and credence in 1985, when the Connecticut state legislature considered a bill to ban the throwing of rice at weddings in order to save bird lives. Its proponents were convinced that rice ingested by birds swells in their stomachs, resulting in certain and painful death.

Not so, says Sibley, who notes that rice must be boiled before it will expand. (Boiled rice at weddings?) "Furthermore," he adds, "all the food that birds swallow is ground up by powerful muscles and grit in their gizzards."

How did the wild story get started? It seems to have spread when a number of dead birds were found on a church lawn in Connecticut. Who knows what killed them? It may have been pesticides or herbicides. The actual cause of death will never be known, but a theory based on creative imagination, unencumbered by scientific information, blamed the fatalities on rice that was left on the ground after a wedding. Easy answers are better than none. The Connecticut bill was introduced in response to the complaints of church officials, and citizens naturally took the bill seriously. Misleading articles in newspapers and magazines helped perpetuate the myth.

Sibley, who has done considerable research on the matter as the myth continues to surface, has found the issue further complicated by evidence of the occasional use of colored and perfumed rice, which might well contain harmful ingredients. It may be ever so chic, but he doesn't recommend it.

How about plain, unadulterated rice? Perfectly harmless, says Sibley. Throw all the rice you like. It will make the birds happy and healthy.

At which point the Rev. Ralph O. Marsh enters the fray, speaking from his stronghold at St. Mary's Chapel in Athens, Georgia. He cringes with horror at the very thought of rice on church steps. His concern is not "little birds' swelling tummies," he confesses. "But I become hysterical when I think of little old ladies who have broken hips as the result of falling on rice spread across already smooth surfaces."

His church bans rice and imposes a financial penalty on anyone who allows it to be used. "The stuff is lethal!" says Rev. Marsh.

How about birdseed? "That could be just as lethal."

Being of the brittle-bone generation, I am in sympathy with the Marsh position. Besides, I've never understood the impulse to throw things at bridal couples. For those who have that compulsion, I say throw nothing but kisses and good wishes. And have a lovely wedding.

GREAT BLUE

A rapturous beginner called to tell me all about his first field trip, one he would always remember.

"And we saw a *great blue heron*," he concluded, in awed tones.

It would have been surprising, given the habitat visited and the time of year, if he had *not* seen a great blue heron. But who would want to detract from the experience by suggesting that this is, after all, a common bird in these parts?

I have taken no polls, but on the basis of many similar reports from beginners who were subsequently hooked on birds, I'm convinced that the great blue heron is responsible for more converts to birdwatching than any other North American bird.

Understandably so. It is the ideal beginner's bird. Unlike the frustrating little warblers that move too fast and hide behind leaves, the great blue stands quietly, right in the open, sometimes motionless for minutes at a time, allowing for close and satisfying scrutiny. Even in flight, when he spreads his wings to their nearly six-foot span, he is easy to identify, easy to describe and, once seen, impossible to forget.

He strikes poses, inviting photographs. From time to time, some photographer for a city newspaper will discover the great blue and produce a full-page spread of portraits, depicting this handsome bird in all his varied aspects: elegant and awkward, regal and comical, rigidly alert and languidly bored.

He is the keen-eyed fisherman, standing stock-still in shallow water, his long neck outstretched, his piercing gaze fixed on a possible meal. He is the dashing suitor, displaying his alluring plumes. He is a clown doing a balancing act on one spindly leg while raising the other to scratch his head. He is a cantankerous old grouch, scrunched down absurdly neckless, like a seedy old man on a park bench with his coat collar turned up against wind and rain.

Whatever the mood or stance, he is impressive.

After the appearance of one of these occasional photo-essays, I can anticipate a flurry of telephone calls from readers who want to know where they can go to see this incredible bird—or perhaps to photograph it for themselves.

One of those calls was as memorable as the bird itself.

The man spoke hesitantly, with a European accent I could not pin to a specific country. The voice was not young, but it held a special note of eagerness that we associate with youth. He referred to the story in *The Washington Post* and asked if I had ever seen great blue herons in the Washington area.

Should I say "hundreds of them"? No, that might sound boastful; even worse, it might have the effect of reducing this extraordinary bird to the ordinary.

I simply confirmed that they do frequent the area.

He sighed. "I have never seen one. From the pictures, I think it is a remarkable bird?" He gave it the inflection of a question, seeking confirmation.

"Unforgettable," I said.

Of course he wanted to know where to find them, and I told him they appear—usually singly, not in flocks—along the Potomac River and the Chesapeake and Ohio Canal, in marshes and ponds, and even at city reservoirs.

"Could I get close enough for a photograph?" he asked, adding modestly that he was not a great photographer, but he had recently bought a 200mm lens and he had hopes of getting a picture that he could send to his cousin in Poland.

"It reminds me so much of the beautiful cranes we saw there when we were boys."

He had not been back for many years, and he didn't know if the cranes were still there or if they had been "wiped out by the encroachment of civilization." But he knew his cousin would remember them.

He spoke wistfully of those far-off days and the thrill of seeing the great flocks in flight. And the sound! He would never forget that sound. Had I ever heard them?

I am not familiar with European cranes, but I told him of the sandhill cranes that migrate through Nebraska, where I have seen them in the thousands and heard their haunting trumpet call, now fixed forever in my memory.

He sighed again, a sigh of nostalgia.

"And does the great blue heron have a similar sound?" he asked hopefully.

It was a pity to disillusion him, but if he was going to track down the great blue, he needed to be prepared for its unexpected, inelegant, bloodcurdling call, utterly unlike the music of cranes. James Michener, in *Chesapeake*, translates the sound as "Kraannk!" But that hardly does justice to the awesome note, which is unreproducible, inimitable, and as unforgettable as the bird's appearance.

I remembered, but did not tell my caller, an incident related by a friend who had taken her granddaughter to spend the summer in their cottage on a quiet cove along the coast of Maine. Delighted with the flocks of dunlin and black-bellied plovers that congregated along the beach, Kim quickly learned to use the spotting scope for better views. One quiet night, she took the scope out to look at the moon. Within minutes she came running back, shaking with terror.

"Grandma!" she cried. "Someone is being *murdered* down in the boathouse!"

It was hard to convince the frightened youngster that the guttural gurgle she had heard was only an alarm sounded by the resident great blue heron, disturbed at his roost, and not the final gasp of a person dying of strangulation.

"It has a terrible voice," I said, "like the sound effects in a murder mystery. But it's a lovely bird."

I hope he got a picture to send to his cousin as a link to their shared boyhood experiences. If he went to the spot I recommended, I'm sure he would have seen at least one great blue, probably several of them, and that should have helped satisfy his yearning for the cranes of Poland and his childhood.

I took care to direct him to an accessible site where he would see the great blues at close range, feeding with other herons and egrets on tidal flats that also attract a variety of shorebirds. He might find a whole new world of birds that he had never known in the Old World; and he might recapture the joy and fascination that still gave a youthful eagerness to his voice when he remembered the cranes.

A VIRTUOSO
AT THE WHITE HOUSE

No mistaking that voice. I'd heard it a hundred times on televised White House press conferences. It was the voice that asked the embarrassing questions, the questions no one else dared ask of the President of the United States:

"Sir, why are you out playing golf so much when the public works program needs your attention?"

"Sir, are you planning to send troops into Lebanon without consulting Congress?"

Brisk, business-like, direct: "This is Sarah McClendon. I have a question for you."

She had said the same words to Harry Truman . . . to Dwight Eisenhower . . . to John F. Kennedy . . . to her fellow Texan, Lyndon Johnson . . . again and again, most persistently, to Richard Nixon . . . and Gerald Ford . . . and Jimmy Carter and Ronald Reagan. And now she had a question for me.

"If you're a columnist," she said, "why aren't you a member of the American News Women's Association?"

I'd never called myself a columnist—after all, I just wrote about birds—and no one had ever asked me such a question before. But trust Sarah McClendon.

"I'll send you an application," she said abruptly, and then proceeded to the real purpose of her call.

She had been at a ceremony on the White House lawn honoring a group of students for achievements in science. The President was holding forth on the complex subject of superconductors and supercolliders.

"And all the while he was talking, there was a bird in the very top of a tree, singing its head off. Here was the President talking about energy, and there was that bird, throwing all *his* energy into a song. And he was drowning out the President!"

This she found highly amusing. She noted several members of the press turning to look at the singer. Secret Service men attending to President Reagan glared at it.

This bird was upstaging the Great Communicator.

Sarah thought she'd write a column about it. But being a conscientious reporter, she had to identify the bird. What was it?

A bird that sings loud and long from the very top of a tree in Washington, D.C., can be none other than a mockingbird. Sarah's description confirmed this.

"It was a long, slender bird."

"With a long tail?"

"Yes, a long tail. And at first he sounded like a redbird, (that, I believe, is Texan for cardinal) but I didn't see any red on him. He was just a plain gray bird. And he went on and on."

Assured that this was a mockingbird imitating a cardinal, *inter alia*, and that it was, as she suspected, proclaiming its territory, Sarah McClendon was ready to write her column for the Texas papers.

"If you can get a column out of it, too, more power to you," she said.

Fair enough. I like nothing better than retelling tales of mockingbirds. I mused upon their foibles as I went out to smear peanut-butter and raisins on the perch appropriated by our resident mockingbird. No other bird dares approach within ten feet of it. He taunts them with his imitations.

I have a theory about mockingbirds. I'm convinced that their mimicry has a practical purpose, that when they imitate, in rapid succession, a robin, a cardinal, a titmouse, a Carolina wren, and a red-eyed vireo, they are, in effect, calling the roll of potential trespassers on their preserve and issuing personal warnings to each and every one. A rough translation might be:

"Now hear this. This tree belongs to me, and only me. Cardinals, keep out! Titmice, keep out! Wrens, keep out! Robins, keep out!" And so on, down the list.

Then again, they may be imitating for the pure enjoyment of demonstrating their versatility. Not all their vocalizations seem related to territorial protection.

My friend Paul Sampson, who has never been known to elaborate on the truth, tells of a mockingbird that sang from his chimney top. Inspired by the song he overhead as he cleaned out the fireplace, Paul began to whistle a few bars from Beethoven's Violin Concerto.

"But I couldn't get it quite right," Paul complained. "I tried two or three times and it always came out wrong."

And what did the mockingbird do to humiliate him?

"He whistled it right back at me—but he did it right!"

I would not question Paul's veracity any more than I would attempt to psychoanalyze the mockingbird on the White House grounds, who began with a cardinal's notes and moved on to a series of repetitive phrases as untranslatable as bureaucratese.

Was he, looking down from his high perch, viewing the President and the assembled audience as intruders on his domain? Was he challenging their very presence? Or was he just practicing new phrases for his varied repertoire? ("Mr. President! Mr. President! . . . No more questions, no more questions.")

Whatever the answer, it was—to some, at least—a welcome diversion, the kind of diversion a president might also welcome under certain conditions. It wouldn't be a bad idea, on nice summer days, to hold press conferences on the White House lawn, where there's always the chance of a helicopter appearing at a critical moment to drown out an embarrassing question. The mockingbird could provide its own brand of distraction and, at the end, a fitting finale in a melodious burst of song.

THERE IS NO SUCH BIRD

Through most of a hot July I puzzled over a mystery bird I never saw.

A woman working in her suburban garden had seen it and, failing to find anything that resembled it in her bird guide, had called for help.

After listening to her description, I could reach only one conclusion: There is no such bird—not in the United States, at least. And in subsequent talks with world-class birders of my acquaintance, I found none who could identify the bird described.

The bird, according to the report, was smaller than a robin and all black except for a white band on its black tail, or, as the ornithologists describe it, a subterminal band. Moreover, it had a habit of hovering over flowers with rapidly beating wings, "like a hummingbird," my informant said.

I considered the possibilities. It could be an escaped cage bird, imported from who-knows-where; it could be a familiar local bird with aberrant plumage; or this could be a case of misperception and inaccurate description, not at all uncommon with amateur observers. That seemed the most likely explanation, and I suspected that this report would end in the UFO file with other Unidentified Flying Objects that had claimed my attention.

Still, the observer was not strictly an amateur. Jean told me when she introduced herself that she had formerly been a ranger in a national park, and although she specialized in deer populations, not birds, she was trained to observe wildlife.

I was sufficiently intrigued to want to see the bird for myself, if only to determine what was wrong in her description. On the assurance that it frequently appeared in the same vicinity, I drove out to meet Jean at her community garden, some 20 miles away. If this turned out miraculously to be some rarity, the 40-mile round trip would be worth-while. In any case, my curiosity would be satisfied.

But I made two trips and spent considerable time prowling around the garden plot without glimpsing the bird. I did see Eastern kingbirds and, recalling their habit of hovering, suggested to Jean that this might be the bird she saw.

"Oh, no," she disclaimed. "I know the kingbirds. They're white underneath. This bird is black above and below. And the tip of its tail is black, not white. And it's smaller than a kingbird."

Back to the books and back to trusted experts. The answer remained the same: There is no such bird.

Then, to compound the mystery, Jean called in some excitement to report that there were two of those birds at the edge of her garden. I left on vacation that day, still baffled. The probability of two identical escapees or two identical mutants was too remote for credibility. The only reasonable conclusion was that the description was wrong in at least one respect. And as I drove away from the scene of the mystery, I was still trying to resolve it to my own satisfaction.

Somewhere along the way, the matter faded from my mind as I traveled in strange territory and struggled to identify mystery birds of my own. But I was reminded of it when, unpacking from vacation, I received a call about another mystery bird.

The man who called let me know that he was telephoning from his car, which seemed to give the matter of identification a certain urgency. I had never before been called from a moving vehicle.

Driving in the country, he had seen a "huge bird" in the road ahead of him, "a dark bird, either black or dark brown." Maybe the transmission from his car telephone was poor, but I understood him to say that the bird was six feet tall.

"Did it have long legs?" I asked.

"I assume so," he said, "but the wings drooped down to cover the legs."

Immediately I had the mental picture of a vulture, a bird that is so graceful in flight, and yet so untidy-looking as it hunches on the ground to feed on a dead carcass by the roadside.

"It looked menacing," the man went on. (Why do people always think vultures look menacing?) He had been concerned for the safety of a boy on a bicycle who had passed quite near the bird. He feared the boy might be attacked or carried off. But fortunately the bird flew up, flapping heavily as if having a hard time getting airborne, spread its monstrous wings, and glided to a landing in the road farther ahead.

All this confirmed my initial impression, and I was confident in informing the man that he had seen a harmless vulture, a bird that feeds on carrion and would never attack a live being.

He was not as confident. I heard the skepticism in his voice as he told me he had sometimes seen vultures overhead, or what he assumed were vultures, and they didn't look that big.

"This was a *big* bird," he reiterated. "Like an eagle, maybe . . ."

His voice trailed off, and I knew without asking that he had never seen an eagle. I knew, too, that he was an inexpert observer whose judgment of relative size and distance could not be trusted. To him, a high-soaring vulture would naturally look small in comparison to a vulture seen close at hand in a moment of surprise.

"Vultures *are* big birds," I assured him. "A turkey vulture has a wingspan of six feet."

"Oh, this was twice that span," he protested, and I had to tell him the undeniable truth about a six-foot bird with a twelve-foot wingspan: "There is no such bird."

Reluctantly, he allowed himself to be persuaded that this startling vision by the roadside was only an ordinary turkey vulture going about its daily life.

Size, I reflected as I left the telephone, is the element most often misjudged by amateur bird observers, but rarely is an observer quite this far from the mark.

That's when I thought again about the mystery bird that hovered, hummingbird style, over a patch of wildflowers growing by a suburban garden. What size was it, really? And did it really beat its wings as rapidly as a hummingbird? It was inconceivable. There was too much wrong with the picture. I was ready to chalk it up to poor observation.

Sometimes the mystery lies not in the bird, but in the eyes of the beholder.

✜
SEE THE BABY HUMMINGBIRDS!

When all the calls are about hummingbirds, I know it has to be August. No other bird is the object of such fascination and curiosity; no other bird is the subject of so many questions.

Each year about this time, when the hummingbirds begin to hover over the powder-puff pink blossoms of our mimosa, I think I should issue a press release composed of typical questions and answers.

Q: What kind of hummingbirds are these coming to my feeder?

A: They are all ruby-throated hummingbirds. That's the only kind we have in the East.

Q: Why don't they have ruby throats?

A: The males do have; the females and young ones do not.

Q: Why don't I ever see any males?

A: This is due partly to luck, partly to the law of averages. Females lay two eggs with each brood and often have two broods in one season, so females and juveniles combined may outnumber adult males five to one. Also, the sexes migrate separately, and the males leave first.

Q: I've planted petunias, and impatiens, and scarlet sage, and I have trumpet vine and fuchsia—but I'm not getting any hummingbirds. How come?

A: That's a tough one. I have only a small bed of impatiens and a mimosa tree, and that seems to be enough to attract hummingbirds. But it's hard to say why a certain bird appears in one back yard and not in another just across the street. However, I wouldn't be so sure that there are no hummers visiting that ideal garden, with all its attractions. They are so small, and they dart in and out so quickly that they could be making frequent forays without being seen. And none of us can keep a constant vigil over our flower gardens.

Q: What is the best mixture to use in a hummingbird feeder?

A: You can buy commercially prepared "nectar," but I make a simple sugar syrup, four parts water to one part sugar. It's wise to boil it to prevent fermentation, and to empty and clean the feeder twice a week in hot weather.

Q: Should I put red dye in the syrup?

A: That isn't necessary. There's enough red on the feeder to attract the hummingbirds' attention.

Q: Do hummingbirds really see color?

A: They certainly do. We put a bright red sculpture out in the garden and watched a male ruby-throat explore it, inch by inch, before giving up and flying on to the feeder. There have been many reports of hummingbirds, attracted by red insulators, meeting their death on electric fences. Substituting green insulators has saved many hummingbird lives.

Q: I'm not seeing as many hummingbirds this year. Are they endangered?

A: There is no doubt that numbers of ruby-throated hummingbirds are declining, but they are not yet on the U.S. Fish and Wildlife Service's Endangered Species List. However, they have been on the National Audubon Society's Blue List since 1978, which indicates that there is cause for concern.

• • •

People are concerned about hummingbirds. They love to watch them, and they want to be helpful. Some are genuinely apprehensive about doing inadvertent harm. More than one person has questioned whether the practice of feeding them sugar-water might be detrimental.

One such caller stated in no equivocal terms that he wanted to talk to an authority on hummingbirds. I don't pretend to be an authority on hummingbirds or anything else. But I have instant access to any number of authorities on my library shelf, and I'm always willing to defer to them on questions I can't answer.

After some hesitation, he decided it was all right to put the question to me. Was it a bad practice to feed hummingbirds? He loved watching them in his yard. But he wanted to do what was in the best interest of the birds, and he had read that there was a danger of making them dependent on this food source, so they would fail to migrate south at the proper time. Was it possible that they would overstay the season and be caught here in a cold wave that they could not possibly survive?

His concern was admirable, and I was happy to be able to ease his conscience with the startling information that migration does not depend on food supply, but on the dictates of a biological time-clock. Hummingbirds vary their diet with nectar from flowers, sap from trees, and a surprising number of spiders, even when they are making regular visits to the backyard feeder. And they migrate on schedule every year, even though there is still an abundance of flowers in gardens and fields to provide them with nectar.

Some people call not to ask questions, but to share interesting observations.

There are those who have just seen their first hummer and are filled with the excitement of discovery. There are others who have taken the time, on a leisurely summer day, to observe the birds closely for the first time and have found that these small, delicate creatures are amazingly pugnacious, willing to attack not only each other but anything that ventures into their orbit, from bumblebees to sharp-shinned hawks.

A man calls from South Carolina to share the news that he has two albino hummingbirds in his yard. He says they are not pure white but a creamy beige, and they behave the same as his other hummingbirds. He has taken pictures, thinking this might be unusual. Albinism in hummingbirds is certainly not common. It is the first report that has come to me, and the *Audubon Encyclopedia of North American Birds*, to which I refer for such information, reports only one albino ruby-throat, recorded in 1953. I tell the caller that one alone is unusual, two together even more so. His pictures, if they are good, will provide the evidence for establishing a new record.

There are always several calls about "baby hummingbirds." These I can predict with certainty, every August. The callers are always so delighted, so eager to share their find.

"I wish you could see my baby hummingbirds," says a woman with a fluttery voice that goes up and down the scale as she reports on the wondrous experience. She was in the garden at dusk when they all came out, a great flock of them, and hovered over her zinnias with their little wings beating a mile a minute. And they didn't seem at all frightened. They were so close she could have reached out and touched them. She could even see their little antennae.

Antennae? That was the tip-off. "A whole flock" of hummingbirds is enough to strain credulity, and "baby hummingbirds," by the time they can fly, are not noticeably different from the adults. But the presence of antennae is irrefutable. Birds don't have antennae.

What she was seeing was a flock of newly-emerged sphinx moths, which hover over flowers much as hummingbirds do. They are so frequently mistaken for hummers that field guides make note of it. Peterson, in his *Field Guide to the Birds East of the Rockies*, even includes a picture of a sphinx moth alongside that of the ruby-throated hummingbird for comparison.

It is not easy to convince the ecstatic lady that her baby hummingbirds are moths. She wants so much for them to be hummingbirds. I refer her to the exact page in the Peterson guide and call her attention to his comment that they "seldom visit flowers before dusk."

That phrase sticks in my mind as I hang up on the disappointed woman. It rings a distant bell.

There was that mystery bird, back in July, that appeared at dusk at the edge of a suburban garden, hovering over a bank of flowers. And then there were two of them. No one had seen them but the woman named Jean who reported them to me, and I had been skeptical of her description. My conclusion had been:

There is no such bird.

Could they have been moths?

The thought had not occurred to me at the time, possibly because I don't usually get sphinx moth reports that early in the season, and because Jean didn't strike me as a totally inexperienced observer.

But her two mystery birds were black, I remind myself, with a white band on the tail. The sphinx moth shown in the Peterson guide is creamy beige—and moths don't have tails. Still, it's worth checking with an entomologist.

What I learn is most intriguing.

Some species of the large sphinx moth (which is also aptly called "the hummingbird moth") are dark. Many of them have tufts of hair at the end of their bodies that resemble a tail. Many also have white or yellow markings at the end of the abdomen that might give the appearance of a banded tail.

On the verge of solving an old mystery, I check the arguments pro and con, guarding against false conclusions. It was significant that the mystery "birds" were always seen at dusk, which was the only time Jean had for gardening after a day's work. But she described them as "smaller than a robin," not "smaller than a hummingbird."

But, as I have often said (and sometimes forget), the one element in a description that is most likely to be wrong is the size. And obviously something was amiss in Jean's description.

One more mystery solved, at least to my satisfaction. I doubt that Jean would accept the solution, but it doesn't matter now.

I take another look at Peterson's creamy-beige sphinx moth with its delicate antennae and its long proboscis probing a tubular flower. Another warning bell rings in my head. I begin to wonder about those two creamy-beige albino hummingbirds down in South Carolina. I wonder what time of day the gentleman saw them—and whether the pictures will reveal antennae.

A NEST IS NOT A HOME

Some people are blessed with the gift of photographic memory. I have auditory memory, which may be an equal asset. I hear sounds in my head with great clarity—not imagined sounds like voices from the heavens, but remembered sounds from as far back as early childhood.

This is a fine thing for birders. It is also a fine thing for pure enjoyment. With no effort, I can hear the song of a robin at any time of the day or year, and I can hear my mother's voice explaining that this incredibly sweet, pure music is the robin's "rain song." These are happy sounds.

By contrast, the memory of the meadowlark's spring song echoing across the pasture is hauntingly wistful. So is my father's clear tenor, singing a song he taught us when we were small, a song called "The Empty Nest." It is not just that I remember the music and words; I can hear them in his voice, and feel again the pang of sorrow induced by the last line:

Now that little empty nest sadly swings alone.

Those sounds from childhood came back to me recently, triggered by a telephone call. A lady who had apparently discovered birds late in life wanted to tell me about her robin.

She had been spending leisure time sitting on her deck and often had the company of a friendly robin that sat on the railing nearby, singing his heart out. He sang day after day, she said, but did not attract a mate. Nevertheless, he began to build a nest in a nearby shrub. Wanting to encourage his efforts, the helpful lady put pieces of string out on the deck. He promptly wove them into the nest. Still no mate came. She put out more string and noted with delight that the discriminating robin used the white string but ignored the red string.

Within a few days the nest was completed and, she reported

with wonder and just a hint of pride, "He's living in it!"

I am constantly amazed by the number of people who have no idea of the function of a bird's nest. Having grown up as I did with parents who explained these things, I can't remember when I first knew that birds build nests for the purpose of having a place to lay and hatch eggs, and to cradle the young until they are big enough to fly. I knew from early childhood that a nest is not a home to which the young would return to visit their parents, or in which the parents would remain and grow old. A nest, for all the care taken in construction, is only temporary housing.

That was the message of "The Empty Nest," and I knew when my father sang it that it was the story of the passing seasons as we had observed them. We were keenly appreciative of "the happy spring," for the Illinois winters were long and harsh and the bitter winds sweeping across the unresistant prairie carried no sound of bird song. The story began in the fall:

In a leafless maple tree, hanging on a bough,
Swings a little empty nest, sad and lonely now . . .

I remembered November winds lashing the branches of the maple tree along the sloping roof outside the dormer window and rocking the nest that we had watched the robins build in early spring, before the leaves were out. The nest was on the same branch that supported our rope swing. Beneath the swing the grass was worn away, and it was here that the robins found worms surfacing after a rain. Here they gathered mud to cement the sturdy nest.

It didn't really "hang" on the bough. That sounded more like the basket-woven oriole nest higher up in the same tree. The robin nest fit snugly in a fork and was not easily dislodged by fierce weather. But I was sure the empty nest of the song was a robin's nest, because it mentioned the "five wee eggs of blue." My brother and I had risked our necks climbing out on the roof to get a closer look at those five blue eggs, and later on to see the naked young birds, hidden from window-side view by a curtain of fresh green maple leaves.

Listening to the narrative of the woman who had taken up robin-watching late in life, I wondered how I could tell her—or if I should tell her at all—these things that I had known practically all my life. Would she be embarrassed? Disappointed?

Truth won out.

"That would be the female sitting on the nest," I said.

"Oh, but he has an orange breast!" she protested.

I don't know what image she had of a female robin, but she was surprised to learn that both sexes have orange breasts—the female is just somewhat lighter, a difference not always noticed by the unpracticed eye.

"I think you have a *pair* of robins there," I went on. "You just haven't seen them both at the same time. The male does the singing, the female does most of the nest-building, then she lays eggs, usually one a day, and keeps them warm until they hatch."

I explained to her about the incubation period and expressed the hope that there were, indeed, two adults to take care of the young robins. The female would have great difficulty as a single parent if anything had happened to the supportive male. In all probability, this being late enough in the season for a second brood, the male was still spending much of his time checking up on the youngsters of the first brood.

The lady was neither embarrassed nor disappointed to learn that her notion of a lonely bachelor robin setting up housekeeping was all wrong. On the contrary, she was excited at the prospect of watching a family of robins grow up before her eyes, within view from her favorite chair on the deck, and I reflected that the discovery of birds can bring equal pleasure to the old and the young.

I told her the eggs would hatch in about two weeks, and the young birds would be ready to fly in 14 to 16 days. I suggested that she note on her calendar the date that the parents first started carrying food to the nest, so she could calculate the date that the fledglings were due to take off. She might witness the event if she kept a close watch at dawn and dusk, the times favored for launching a family of robins.

If anything disappointed her, it was the knowledge that once they were gone they would not come back—none of them. The adults might well turn their attention immediately to raising a third brood in a new nest. The youngsters would be essentially homeless, fending for themselves and, later, joining with flocks to migrate south. The nest that had cradled them would no longer be a shelter from storms. It would have no sentimental attachment for them.

Only for humans is the image of the empty nest a poignant one. I'm sure it was to my father. I can hear it in his young voice as he sings in my ear:

Now those happy days are gone, all the birds have flown.
Now that little empty nest sadly swings alone.

shafer

MYSTERIES OF AUTUMN

The dog days of summer melt away in their own heat, and the sun shows signs of early retirement. The tempo of life accelerates. Birders feel the electricity of change in the air long before the first blush is on the maples. Even in our sleep we hear the fluttering of a thousand wings, and we wake full of expectancy, ready for that most remarkable and mysterious natural phenomenon called migration. The summer residents move out, and great flocks of waterfowl move in for the winter. In this season of arrivals and departures, who knows what strangers may pass our way?

Here on Melody Lane, we watch the massing of robins and hear the taunting cries of blue jays. Small warblers flit silently through the trees. This is not the season for their song.

The telephone rings . . .

MIGRATION ANXIETY

September was finally asserting itself after a week of insufferable domination by weather more fitting for July. Throwing the windows wide to welcome the first cool breeze of autumn, I heard a steady series of insistent chips. Outside, patient cardinal parents were responding to the demands of three hungry, dingy youngsters, their third brood of the year.

They deserved a helping hand. Breaking with past precedent, I put out some sunflower seeds, and by that act I knew I was making a commitment to daily feeding, pushing the calendar forward into October, the month when our feeding stations normally open.

The act was accompanied by a certain anxiety. Call it my "migration neurosis." I always worry a little about the coming season, wondering whether it will bring massive waves or a disappointing trickle, like last spring's migration which, according to all reports up and down the East Coast, had been disturbingly low in numbers and species. Because of that dismal record, there was an increased anxiety about the fall prospects.

As I scattered seeds on the ground and watched the house finches gather to compete with the cardinals, I was mulling over the first telephone call of the day. A friend who had spent the summer on her farm reported in dismay: "But there were no birds!" She had especially missed her favorite phoebes. They used to be "all over the place," but this year brought only one pair.

It was a familiar lament. Alarm notes had been sounding long before the disastrous spring migration. As early as February, anxious feeder-watchers were calling to ask where the birds were, reinforcing my own concerns. It had not been a normal season, in my back yard or anywhere in the immediate area. Except for the ever-growing numbers of house finches, we were seeing fewer of all the familiar winter residents: fewer cardinals and blue jays, fewer juncos, and practically no white-throated sparrows. Where we used to entertain 20 white-throats at a time, they were appearing only singly or, at best, in pairs.

We searched for possible reasons. Could it be simply a matter of distribution? Sales of birdseed indicate that far more people are maintaining feeding stations in recent years, so it is logical to conclude that the birds have scattered to new supply sources. Good news, if true; but this is only speculation, supported by admittedly unscientific observations that, out in the field, there did not appear to be a significant decline in numbers.

And yet there was an uneasiness.

The uneasiness grew when spring migration fizzled out. Bird-banders and birders compared notes. Where were all the songbirds? What had happened to the warblers? The annual May Count produced low numbers, in species and individuals. It was the worst birding season in memory.

Then in June, when the summer residents had settled down, came an especially poignant call from a stranger.

"I'm an old codger," he introduced himself, adding by way of proof, "I've just come back from my 60th-year class reunion at Yale."

Congratulations were in order. But he was not soliciting congratulations. What he wanted was information—and perhaps reassurance.

After visiting his old campus, he had gone to see his brother in the Poconos in Pennsylvania, where they had grown up. One of the pleasures he remembered from boyhood days was the chorus of birds at dawn and dusk, with the music of thrushes filling the air.

But this year there was no chorus.

What had happened? Had there been a sharp decline in songbird populations? Had Rachel Carson's "silent spring" really come to pass?

Sadly, I thought that a man in his eighties might not hear as well as he did at eight or eighteen. I took this into account, without offering it as an explanation. But at the same time there was the chilling reminder that this summer, for the first time in 14 years, the song of the wood thrush was missing here on Melody Lane.

I could offer neither reassurance nor solid information. The truth is, we don't know and cannot know except in retrospect whether we're in a natural cycle or an irreversible plunge. I wondered if people once talked about the passenger pigeons the way we were now talking of thrushes.

We look for hopeful signs even as we remember Rachel Carson's predictions, even as we read of the inexorable destruction of songbird habitat in the tropical rain forests, where they spend the winter.

There might be logical, less ominous, reasons for the thin spring migration. Perhaps it is due in part to an unseasonably warm spring and trees fully leafed out before the migrants arrived, concealing them in dense foliage. Perhaps the weather had not been conducive to any great waves, and the birds had filtered through in a diffuse, less perceptible movement. Perhaps the fly-by-night migrants had passed over us on a favorable wind without touching down by day.

Conjecture, all conjecture. But we take comfort from reports of good numbers banded at stations west of the mountains, suggesting that many migrants, for some mysterious reason, may have taken an unaccustomed inland route.

What is the evidence to the north? Were there as many breeding birds on territory as usual?

Walking in a New Brunswick forest in early July, I was heartened to see and hear all the warblers I had missed in migration: magnolia, Cape May, bay-breasted, black-throated green, mourning, and Nashville, all in good numbers, and Tennessees so abundant that their songs were overwhelming.

But this is only a tiny sampling, the inexpert impression of an ignorant observer on a first-time visit to that region, one who has no idea of how many birds to expect. What is the broader picture?

At the Patuxent Wildlife Research Station, the experts on migratory birds have no answers. They do not collect statistics on the breeding populations in Canada. But they caution against drawing unfounded conclusions. There is no correlation, they say, between the spring and fall migrations. It can be heavy this fall, thin next spring. There are too many variables: breeding success, food supply, weather conditions, shrinking of habitat.

I thought of all these things and I thought of cycles as I watched the cardinals, which raised three broods this year instead of their usual two. They were joined in the back yard by families of chickadees, titmice, and house finches, all lured by the early windfall of sunflower seed. The yard was suddenly alive with birds.

On the ground were six song sparrows, the two adults feeding four fledglings. They, too, had three broods this year. The catbirds, who usually have only one, raised two broods. So did the barn swallows across the street. So did the Carolina wrens. Hearing their calls ringing through the woods, I remembered when Carolina wrens were all but wiped out by three vicious winters in succession, and I found encouragement in contemplating nature's cycles.

Maybe this year the white-throated sparrows will make just such a comeback. Maybe next year we will have wood thrushes again.

I felt a surge of optimism as my eyes fixed on a slight quiver in an azalea bush and watched it develop into a juvenile magnolia warbler, emerging from the greenery to herald the beginning of another migration.

It takes so little to gladden the heart of a birder.

ADDRESS: ATLANTIC FLYWAY

Real estate advice? That's hardly my line. But here was a prominent realtor calling with a serious problem.

It took me by surprise, although it shouldn't have. I've become accustomed to calls that I put in the "non-ID" category, calls from a cross-section of citizens who don't need to have a bird identified but do need information relating to birds in general. Naturally, they reach for the telephone book and look up the Audubon Society.

Already I had had three "non-ID" calls in one day.

The first came from an artist who was working on a ceramic sculpture of our state bird, the Baltimore (northern) oriole. She had the design clearly in mind. She wanted to portray the bird alighting on a branch, wings outspread. The trouble was, she had never seen an oriole, and the only pictures she found in field guides showed the bird with wings folded. In the interest of accuracy, she needed to know: "What color is the underside of the wing? Is it black, like the top of the wing, or is it orange like the body?" (Answer: It is a yellowish-orange, paler than the body.)

The next caller was a young man who wanted to know the best time to go to Blackwater National Wildlife Refuge to see the geese and swans coming in. (Canada and snow geese arrive in good numbers in October, but it's best to wait until mid-November if you want to see tundra swans.)

Before the realtor called, I had just dealt with a young woman desperately searching for a purple martin house—this on an autumn day when all the purple martins were well on their way to South America. It didn't make sense until she explained that she was the props manager for an amateur theatre group, and this was on her "must" list for their next production. I put her in touch with George Petrides, the accommodating owner of the

Wild Bird Center, who had a martin house in stock that he was glad to lend for the duration of the play.

Then came the real estate lady. She had a prestigious client, she explained, a British bird artist who was planning to spend a couple of years painting the birds of North America. He had engaged her to find a house that would be appropriate for an operating base—to buy or lease, he wasn't particular. He was particular about only one thing: It had to be "on the flyway."

She had accepted the assignment by transatlantic telephone without admitting her ignorance, which she now revealed to me in a plea for guidance. "Where is the flyway?"

She sounded embarrassed, heaven knows why. There was no more reason for her to know about the comings and goings of birds than for me to know about the day-to-day fluctuations of mortgage interest rates. Still, I found it somewhat amusing—in the same category with the question I get every year from earnest amateurs and from journalists assigned to do a feature story on bird migration. As if expecting road-map directions to a specific point, they ask: "Where can I go to see the migration?"

They are unaware that "the migration" occurs all over the United States, at varying times for different species. Birds are not restricted to any narrow corridors of passage. But the U.S. Fish & Wildlife Service has designated four major routes followed by migratory birds as they travel between their nesting grounds and their winter residences: the Pacific Flyway, along the west coast; the Central Flyway, over the Great Plains; the Mississippi Flyway, following the river; and the Atlantic Flyway in the east.

None of these have sharply defined borders. The Atlantic Flyway (where the British artist wanted to locate) is a broad swath stretching from the Atlantic coast westward to the Allegheny Mountains. So, technically, my home is on the flyway. So is the office of the realtor who was seeking my advice. But usually when people speak of the flyway, they are referring to the route taken by waterfowl, the thousands of migratory ducks, geese, and swans that winter along the Atlantic Coast. Great numbers of them concentrate on the Delmarva Peninsula, where there are a number of hospitable refuges to accommodate them.

So if the British artist was interested in waterfowl, a location on Maryland's Eastern Shore near Chesapeake Bay would be ideal—at least from October, when the flocks begin to arrive in V-formation squadrons, until April, when they return to northern Canada and Alaska for the nesting season. Following their exodus, shorebirds move through in impressive numbers, and the picturesque waders—herons and egrets—arrive for the summer. With the added attraction of gulls and terns, the Eastern Shore is a lively enough place to keep bird artists and photographers happily engaged.

But if the artist was more interested in songbirds, he could be just as happy right here in Montgomery County, Maryland. Along the Potomac River and the Chesapeake and Ohio Canal, he would find an abundance of songbirds, including a great variety of the colorful warblers that always amaze British birders, accustomed as they are to very drab warblers which, like our Empidonax flycatchers, are almost impossible to distinguish except by song. Some of the more spectacular warblers spend their summers and rear their young here: the yellow-throated, the parula, the prairie, and the legendary prothonotary.

We have bluebirds and blue jays and blue grosbeaks; orioles and cardinals and American robins (so unlike the English robin). We have swallows and wrens and, as the commercials say, much, much more.

I have counted 99 species without ever leaving our property. Today, between phone calls, I have seen from my window a Swainson's thrush, a female yellowthroat, a pair of American redstarts, and magnolia, chestnut-sided, and Cape May warblers, all migrants. Nighthawks have already passed through. I have seen ospreys heading south on solo flights and broad-winged hawks moving in leisurely spirals, 50 or 60 at a time.

We were not aware of all these advantages when we bought this house on Melody Lane. We made no special stipulations to the real estate agent, other than finding us a comfortable home in a convenient location. But luck was with us.

We remember our good fortune every year about this time. Any day now, we may awake to hear the haunting chorus of geese overhead, reminding us that we have a very good address, right on the Atlantic Flyway.

THE WHISTLER

She calls herself Miss Thomas, and she calls often enough that I have learned to recognize her voice, often enough that she might reasonably introduce herself by first name, as many strangers do. She enunciates carefully. It is clearly "Miss," not "Ms."

In my mind I call her "The Whistler." Not that she whistles well. She whistles rather poorly. But she has a great curiosity about bird calls and will try valiantly to reproduce them so that I can identify them.

In the beginning I asked her, "What does the bird look like?" But I stopped asking that. I learned that her curiosity didn't impel her to take the fairly obvious step of searching out the bird that went with the voice.

"I don't know," she said at first. "I never see the bird. I just *hear* it all day."

Our acquaintance began with a mockingbird, which was fairly easy to identify although she couldn't begin to match his virtuoso performance. But even a poor imitation, coupled with the information that the bird sang not only all day but also in the middle of the night, was all I needed to be sure.

I encouraged her to go out and look for a gray bird with white wing patches, a bird that has the habit of singing from the highest available perch and, in mid-song, throwing himself into the air in an apparent burst of exuberance. But I don't think she followed my advice. It was as if I had identified Beethoven's Sixth for her; once she had a title to go with the music, she was satisfied.

Her goldfinch imitation was more difficult. She repeated it several times, with great perseverance and assurance. Finally she offered further information.

"They must be quite common," she insisted. "I hear several of them calling at once, in the direction of my neighbor's sunflowers."

Maybe Miss Thomas had some visual problem, I thought, not to have noticed the bright yellow goldfinches bouncing about among the sunflowers to harvest their seeds. It would have been indelicate to ask.

On another occasion, she did a passable imitation of the white-throated sparrow's "Poor Sam Peabody" and then whistled the familiar "fee-bee, fee-bay" that is popularly known among birders as "the chickadee's love-song." It surprised Miss Thomas to learn that these clear, sweet notes came from the same bird that utters the distinctive but unmusical "chicka-dee-dee-dee." This she had heard many times, and in fact she knew chickadees by sight.

So she did know some birds, after all.

She knew robins, of course, but somehow had never connected them with the "cheerily, cheerily" song that she whistled to me on a rainy day. She was delighted with the discovery and thanked me graciously, as she did with each call.

It occurred to me to suggest that she could buy recordings of bird songs to help her put names to the ones she heard, but on second thought I refrained. I didn't want her to think I objected to these occasional calls. And I had begun to suspect, without knowing a thing about her circumstances, that Miss Thomas was rather lonely.

A month or so passed before I heard from her again. Returning from a trip, I found a letter from her in the accumulated mail, signed with her full name preceded by the customary "Miss."

"I have been trying for several days to reach you," she wrote in a neat, precise hand, "but getting no answer, I think you must be out of town. I have two birds for you to identify. One goes, 'whistle, whistle, chop-chop-chop,' and the other one calls all day long, the same two notes, repeated three times. I think he is saying, 'wheedle, wheedle, wheedle,' or possibly 'fee-bee, fee-bee, fee-bee.' I'm not sure.

"If you would be good enough to call me when you get back, I could try to whistle them for you. Thank you."

Before calling The Whistler, I studied her verbal renditions and decided that "whistle, whistle, chop-chop-chop" must be the cardinal (surely she must have heard it many times before this!), and that the repetitive two-note call had to be that of the tufted titmouse, which is frequently translated as "Peter, Peter, Peter."

Miss Thomas was greatly relieved to hear from me and especially pleased that I was able to name her two mystery birds with some confidence. She had indeed seen the beautiful cardinals, she said, but she did not know the tufted titmouse. She would look it up in the book.

"I bought a bird book while you were away," she announced proudly. "I don't know why I never got one before. I have a lot of books. I've always read a great deal."

And in a rush of unaccustomed confidentiality, she went on to say, "I'm alone, you know. I've never married. But I hope to someday," she added cheerfully. "I haven't given up. In the meantime, I have my books . . . and the birds."

"It's nice to talk to you," I said. "Call me if you have any more mysteries."

Outside, our Carolina wren, which sings in all seasons, was doing his best to dispel the gloom of the bleak, gray day. In the face of a disagreeable northeast wind with forebodings of winter, he still sounded cheery and optimistic. It is true, I think, that hope springs eternal, in wrens and in other whistlers.

AN INVASION OF SWIFTS

It would not be a normal autumn without at least one telephone call about chimney swifts. Many people mistake them for bats and become alarmed over what they perceive as a great and menacing swarm of bats disappearing into a chimney.

Swifts are quite distinctive, with their cigar-shaped bodies and slender, pointed wings. They have an unusual style of flight. My husband says it looks as if they had just passed through a shower and are shaking water off their wings.

In September we sometimes see migrating flocks of hundreds or even thousands circling over a chimney that they have chosen as a stopover on their route to South America, and it's fascinating to see them gather from all directions to converge on a rendezvous point. The ritual usually begins about dusk, with the ever-expanding flock circling endlessly, as if in indecision. Then, as the sky darkens, the disorganized flock suddenly turns into a compact stream. As if at a signal, they pour into the chimney in a matter of seconds.

There is an aura of mystery about swifts. As a child I found them a source of great wonderment. They were always in motion, never alighting in trees or on wires like other birds. When did they rest? Where did they find food? I knew they nested in the tall chimney of an abandoned brick kiln in our town, but I could never believe that even such a tall chimney could hold so many swifts.

I wondered what the swifts would do if there were no chimneys, and I got an answer to the unspoken question when the chimney was razed in a great jumble of bricks that fell all the way across the road. At dusk the swifts were back, circling round and round over the empty lot, thrown into total confusion. It was the fall migration season, and for several days flocks of varying sizes appeared and swarmed high above the debris. Then they all suddenly disappeared from sight. The swifts did not return to that spot in spring. By some mysterious system of communication, the news had been spread that another chimney had been removed from their landscape.

Of course there were swifts long before there were chimneys, and they found accommodations in hollow trees, as they still do on occasion. I once watched the nightly descent of a flock of migrating swifts into the cavity of an ancient oak tree, which was also inhabited by a raccoon. It must have been startling for the raccoon to have his home invaded by that great flurry of birds, but he seemed to find some entertainment in sitting at the opening and batting at them as they swooshed past him.

Each year someone from the Washington area calls to disclose a new location, often right in the city, where migrant swifts are gathering. One young man, watching a flock he estimated at 5,000 disappear into a smokestack on Connecticut Avenue, called to propose that he be lowered into the smokestack to photograph them on location—if the Audubon Society would provide the camera and equipment. I suggested that this might be an appropriate mission for one of the intrepid photographers of the National Geographic Society.

It was well into October when I got a long distance call from Kevin Jepson, who identified himself as a reporter for a newspaper in Huntington, West Virginia, where the Highlawn Baptist Church was under a siege of swifts.

Residents had observed "thousands of swifts" circling over the church on Sunday afternoon. And then suddenly worshippers heard a great flapping of wings and discovered the birds flying through the church halls, blackening the walls with soot from the chimney, and terrifying some of the more timid, who compared it to the horror of a Hitchcock movie. Predictably, many of them believed these were bats and, under the misapprehension that all bats carry rabies, panicked.

Calmer souls discovered that the confused birds had poured into the church through chimney vents in the boiler room and could not find their way out.

By the time Kevin Jepson arrived on the scene, local Audubon volunteers were on hand, capturing the docile swifts 50 at a time in grocery bags and releasing them. The rescue operation continued into the next day before all the birds, some 1400 of them, were rounded up. Kevin had watched while volunteers banded a number of the swifts. In fact, he had held one in his hand and was completely captivated. It weighed only an ounce, he said, and it was very soft and non-resistant.

For his own information as well as for the follow-up story he planned to write, he wanted to know more about swifts. He assumed they were migrating, but where were they going?

They were headed for Peru, I told him, a fact that was long unknown to ornithologists. In fact, the destination of these travelers was something of a mystery, leading to popular speculation that the birds hibernated. During the 1930s, more than 500,000 swifts were banded in the United States, but no bands were recovered to give a clue to their migration route and final destination.

The riddle was solved in 1943, when Indians coming in to a mission in Peru were seen wearing unique necklaces made from strange silver beads—which proved on closer examination to be neither silver nor beads. They were aluminum leg-bands, each bearing an identifying number and the message: "Write Bird-Band, Washington, D.C. USA."

Kevin wondered whether the occurrence at Highlawn Baptist Church was unusual. I could only say that it was the first time I had heard of a flock of swifts getting trapped in a church. I have noticed that migrating swifts often choose church chimneys for overnight stops. I can't explain this choice, but it may be that the steeples attract their attention as they seek available chimneys.

There was talk, Kevin said, of covering the chimney with screen wire to prevent a recurrence. Remembering the swifts at the old brick kiln, I urged him to prevail on the good church people to put the screen wire over the vents in the boiler room and leave the chimney open in hospitality. Being creatures of habit, the swifts are likely to return by the same route next year. If they do, I hope they find sanctuary at the Highlawn Baptist Church in Huntington.

THE ACCIDENTAL CURLEW

The day had begun with a series of ho-hum calls—routine questions and routine answers. Then Joanna Windsor called, and the tempo changed.

"I've seen the weirdest bird," she began, after introducing herself.

Nothing unusual about that. Many calls begin exactly the same way, and few lead to anything surprising. What appears weird or strange to a non-birder may turn out to be as ordinary as an immature starling or a molting cowbird.

Joanna admitted she is a non-birder. She doesn't even own a field guide. But she is a good observer and she has what I call a "high CQ." It was her Curiosity Quotient that moved her to call the Audubon Society. She simply had to know the name of that bird.

It was not an ordinary bird, I soon realized, and Joanna was not an ordinary amateur observer. She gave a meticulously detailed description of the bird, including all the essential clues of behavior and habitat.

She and her husband Paul had seen it, she said, on the athletic field of the local high school where they had gone to watch a Sunday afternoon game of softball. They—and apparently only they—had taken note of this strange bird feeding in the grass at the edge of the field.

It was a beautiful brown bird, she said, with long legs "and the longest bill I've ever seen on a bird." It was the long, down-curved bill that made the bird look so weird—that and the size of its head, so small in proportion to the oval body, which she judged to be "about the size of one of the biggest seagulls."

Amazed at her detailed observations, I was even more amazed to learn that she was referring, as she talked, to the sketch she had made. Rare is the birder who makes sketches on the spot!

And here was a non-birder, setting a good example for us all. Joanna's sketch had been critiqued by Paul, who reminded her to add the speckling on the back. "He grew up on a farm; he notices those things," she said.

They had gone back after the game to see if the bird was still there. By that time the field had been taken over by a family exercising a pair of Dobermans. The bird, still busily feeding, was not intimidated by the dogs. But Joanna was.

"The bird seemed so tame," she said. "I think I could have gone out and picked it up. But I wasn't about to tangle with those Dobermans."

It was frustrating for them. The library was closed. The Windsors didn't know anyone who knew about birds or owned a field guide. And they couldn't call the Audubon Society until Monday morning. She was tremendously relieved when she finally reached me. Did I have any idea what her mystery bird was?

I had a very good idea. It had to be either a whimbrel or a long-billed curlew. Either would be unusual and worth the hundred-mile round trip to Brandywine . . . if the bird was still there.

Joanna would be only too happy to go and look for it.

Awaiting her call, I mulled over the possibilities. If it was a whimbrel, it was in unusual habitat. Common enough along the coast in fall migration, the whimbrel prefers sandy beaches and mudflats, where it feeds on small mollusks and crustaceans.

A long-billed curlew would be more at home on a grassy ball field, but it would be very far from its normal range west of the Mississippi River. I had seen them in California and on the Central Plains of Manitoba in nesting season. But my sharpest recollection was of the great numbers of long-billed curlews I had seen on an early-spring trip to Texas. They seemed to be everywhere. On the campus of Corpus Christi State College, they were strolling about as tame as chickens. That tallied with Joanna's description: "It seemed so tame."

I waited anxiously for her report. Who knew how long the bird had been there already, or how long it might stay?

It was still there, still feeding quietly, even though the football team was practicing and there was a lot of noise and activity. The bird flew up once and Joanna was afraid it was leaving, but it just circled the field and flew right back to the same spot.

"There must be something special that attracts it to that field," she said.

There was an abundance of crickets, for one thing. When Ted and I arrived on the scene with scope and camera, we were able to get close enough to the bird to see it probing into the turf with that preposterous beak and coming up with large, luscious crickets. From our post at the chain-link fence surrounding the athletic field, we could even see with our binoculars the sensor device at the end of the curved bill that made it possible for the curlew to locate its prey.

Word of the rarity was spread swiftly through the efficient, unofficial birders' network. On the basis of a report by an amateur, a non-birder, veterans hurried to Brandywine. They came from Baltimore and Washington and Annapolis and points between and beyond. They carried binoculars and scopes and high-powered cameras to record the historic event.

Joanna, delighted to have "her bird" identified and appreciated, marveled at the excitement her call had generated. Somehow she had known that this was something special, but she had no idea it was such a rarity, or that so many people would be interested.

Birders came and went. The curlew posed cooperatively and continued to feed sedately, undisturbed by all the attention and equally undisturbed by the football team that often shared its field. It had been sharing that field in pre-season practice sessions even before school opened. The custodian who mowed the grounds reported having seen it sometime in late August. It had followed him, no doubt picking up insects stirred up by the mower, but he had thought nothing of it and hadn't mentioned it to anyone.

The curlew put Brandywine High School on the map. Reporters came and interviewed birders, football players, and the principal. The students elected the long-billed curlew their school mascot and issued bulletins on its daily whereabouts . . . and finally, on its disappearance from the scene after a sojourn of at least three weeks.

Joanna grieved over her bird, worried about its fate. Where would it go from here? Was it doomed to be a lone wanderer, never to find a mate or link up with others of its kind? That was the only logical assumption for a bird so far off its natural course.

Questions abounded. What had brought the bird here in the first place? Joanna had an answer for that one. It was destiny. By the magic of fate, the lost, disoriented bird had been guided straight to Joanna's home territory in order to find a kindred spirit. Like the curlew, Joanna had a poor sense of direction. Paul joked that she could get lost two blocks from home. It was no laughing matter. Joanna knew how it was with the curlew. She kept hoping it would find its way back into her life.

There were no more reports.

How many long-billed curlews have visited Maryland? No one really knows. According to records, Joanna's bird was only the fourth of its kind ever seen in the state; only the second in this century. Previous sightings were as far apart as 1843, 1899, and 1976.

Those are the verified records.

But how many have passed through unnoticed? I always wonder that when a rare bird is spotted.

In The Field List of the Birds of Maryland, the long-billed curlew is one of a select group known as "Accidentals," an intriguing term that invites dual interpretation.

By what accident do these birds appear here at such infrequent intervals, so far from their customary range? And by what accident are they observed by someone who attaches enough significance to the sighting to report it?

Dozens of people must have seen the weird-looking bird with the long, curved bill strolling about the field behind Brandywine High School—and having seen it, must have gone about their affairs without remarking on it. Only one person had made a telephone call.

Joanna had been thinking of taking up birdwatching. Already she had the beginning of a distinguished life-list, with the long-billed curlew right at the top.

✛

THE BIRD IS
QUICKER THAN THE EYE

Indian summer is so confusing, coming along just as we've adjusted to the idea that winter is in the wings.

In bursts of energy we spent those first cool autumn days stacking firewood, bringing in house plants, cleaning and filling the bird feeders, and washing the windows to give us a spotless view of the snow that would soon fall.

Then came a series of warm, drowsy days that sapped our energy and threw everything out of gear.

Even plant and animal life was confused. Forsythia and japonica bloomed. Mockingbirds and cardinals sang serenades to a false spring, and woodpeckers began their ritualistic drumming as if the mating season had overtaken them without benefit of winter's chill.

My telephone rang with springtime complaints from unhappy homeowners, the callers ranging from baffled to furious. Woodpeckers had gone amok, attacking houses instead of trees, drilling holes in shutters and clapboard sidings, startling residents out of their sleep at dawn, sometimes inflicting costly damage.

Like a taped recording, I reiterated the standard advice: Cover the hole with shiny metal, such as a coffee-can lid; hang fluttering streamers near the drill site; and if this fails, buy a plastic owl at a garden shop and perch it in a prominent place on the roof or a window ledge where it will serve to intimidate the marauders. I might have added, "Take two aspirin and call me next week if the woodpecker is still hammering." With the passing of Indian summer, biological clocks would resume normal function and the first frost would chill the ardor of the most zealous of woodpeckers.

Breaking the monotony of the complaint season, there came

an intriguing call from Carl Bode, professor of literature at the University of Maryland. I had never met Dr. Bode, but I was familiar with his poetry and essays.

In scholarly tones he informed me that he had a mockingbird that was behaving like a woodpecker. It had drilled a sizable hole in the cedar siding of his campus home. His resourceful wife had stuffed the hole with aluminum foil to discourage the bird—but they still heard the mockingbird at work, pecking on the outer wall.

Was this a sign of an insect infestation in the cedar? And what could they do to prevent further damage—from insects, mockingbird, or both?

Crazy things happen in Indian summer, but the idea of a mockingbird attacking woodwork was beyond the bounds of credibility. The mockingbird anatomy is not designed for clinging to the trunk of a tree or the side of a house, and the beak is not designed for drilling.

I didn't communicate these thoughts to Dr. Bode. I simply told him this was a mystery that called for on-site investigation. It was a nice day for a drive out to College Park, and the incident offered an opportunity to meet the distinguished author, whose writing I admired.

Parking in front of the cedar frame house, I was greeted first by the prime suspect in the case, singing innocently from the television antenna, then by the plaintiff, who met me on the front steps.

Dr. Bode hardly needed to point out the hole in the wood, slightly above eye level and highlighted by a wad of shiny foil.

This was no feeble amateurish effort, I observed. The hole, three inches in diameter, was clearly the work of a skilled and persistent operator. It could not possibly have been executed by an eccentric mockingbird in a fit of caprice.

Gently, politely, Dr. Bode refuted my verdict with the eyewitness account of Mrs. Bode, who soon joined us to confirm it.

They had heard the tapping, off and on, for several days and had assumed it was made by the little downy woodpecker who frequented the copper beech just in front of the house. When they discovered the freshly-drilled hole in the cedar siding only a few feet from the front door, the matter became serious. They set up a vigil, determined to catch the perpetrator in the act and let him know of their displeasure.

Alerted by the familiar tapping sound, Mrs. Bode had flung open the front door and to her great surprise saw not a woodpecker but a mockingbird! There was no question of its identity: a gray bird with a long tail and white wing patches. And as final proof she offered the clinching evidence: "It flew up, landed on the chimney, and began to sing!"

A very unwoodpecker-like performance, I had to agree.

Subsequently the brazen bird, undeterred by the foil trick, had begun new drills adjacent to the old one, causing understandable concern. The bird usually worked on a sunny afternoon such as this one.

I was invited to come in, have a cup of tea, and wait for the action to begin. I would soon see for myself.

With ears tuned for the telltale signal, we talked quietly of birds in general and of obnoxious woodpeckers in particular. Commiserating with the Bodes, I shared the story of David Brinkley's lament to the Audubon Society that woodpeckers had inflicted $8,000 worth of damage on his home. The Bodes' problem was negligible by comparison—although I refrained from saying so. I also refrained from mentioning the experience of a friend of mine whose home was besieged by a pileated woodpecker with such devastating results that, as a last resort, she had the persistent pileated targeted by a hired gun. And who could blame her? The powerful pileated, I surmised, could in five minutes accomplish more than a downy woodpecker could manage in a full day's work.

I was still convinced that the hole in the Bodes' house had

been made by a downy. They were still convinced that the mockingbird had done it. We waited for proof positive.

With the second round of tea, uninterrupted by any suspicious outdoor noise, Dr. Bode apologized for taking up my time in what might be a futile vigil.

"I'm addicted to mysteries," I confessed. "I can't bear to leave one unsolved."

Dr. Bode admitted that he, too, was fond of mysteries—especially the kind that take place in quiet English villages. He took delight in sifting the clues and predicting the outcome.

After some discussion of our favorite fictional detectives, I suggested that we revisit the scene of the crime in question.

Outside, like Hercule Poirot using "the little gray cells" of the brain to solve the riddle, I suggested this scenario:

Suppose there are two birds—the mockingbird, who sits on the chimney and guards his territory, ready to give chase to any intruder; and the downy woodpecker, who lurks in the copper beech near the door and makes frequent forays to drum a mating call on the side of the house.

Now suppose this noise attracts the attention of Mrs. Bode inside the house and, at the same time, that of the mockingbird on the roof. The mockingbird, true to his nature, zooms down to rout the woodpecker, who takes refuge in the dense foliage of the nearby beech, and Mrs. Bode opens the door just in time to see the mockingbird fly up to sing his victory song from a high perch.

My scenario was consistent with the characters of the two birds and with the well-known axiom that the bird is often quicker than the eye. But I'm not sure the Bodes accepted it without reservation.

Later, I sought the advice of Dr. Donald Messersmith, doubly valuable because he is both entomologist and ornithologist. Speaking entomologically, he discussed the insect-resistant qualities of cedar, which makes it a popular material for closet linings and old-fashioned hope chests. He thought it highly unlikely that the cedar siding of the Bodes' home would suddenly, after 20 insect-free years, be subject to infestation. Speaking ornithologically, Dr. Messersmith endorsed my view that the deed had been done by an ardent woodpecker. He, too, had observed that unseasonal weather had produced peculiar effects on the woodpecker community. They were drumming for love, not for food, when they attacked all those houses.

He rejected unequivocally the theory of mockingbird-turned-woodpecker, in any kind of weather.

I passed the reassuring words on to Dr. Bode, who was having the pockmarks in his house patched and treated with distasteful substances. I don't think he had completely abandoned his original hypothesis. He continued for several days to keep watch and to collect evidence (a feather dropped near the scene of the crime, carefully wrapped in tissue and tucked in an envelope as Exhibit A), and we had pleasant telephone conferences about the mystery, even after I considered it solved.

Then a northwest wind came through in the night, shriveling the forsythia blossoms and icing over the birdbath, and there were no more calls about aberrant woodpeckers. Or mockingbirds.

✣
A BIRD IN A SHROUDED CAGE

Birdwatching is a poor form of exercise, consisting mainly of standing and staring. On a good day, you may stand in one spot for half an hour without moving any part of the anatomy except the finger that adjusts the focus on your binoculars. Elsewhere, muscular atrophy sets in.

So, with high resolve and the best of intentions, I enrolled in a twice-a-week exercise class.

I missed the first class. I made the mistake of answering the telephone.

It should have been safe enough. It was nearly an hour before class time and most calls, even bird calls, can be held to less than ten minutes. But you never know . . .

I recognized the name and the worried voice of Betty Conner, who had called the day before about a hawk in a hurry that had flown right through the screen on her porch and couldn't find its way out. She had not witnessed the mishap, but she had found the hawk on the floor and a jagged hawk-sized hole at the top of the screen. There were crows in the neighborhood making a great racket, and we speculated that they had been in hot pursuit of the hawk when he crashed trying to escape them.

"That hawk is still here," Betty said.

No wonder she was worried. The captive hawk had partaken of neither food nor drink since she first discovered him.

"I did as you said—put chunks of meat and a pan of water just outside and left the screen door open. But he's still on the porch, and I don't think he's had a bite. Do you think he could be brain-damaged?" she asked anxiously.

Why brain-damaged? I wondered. Stunned, possibly, from the impact of the screen. But that was temporary.

"Is he still moving around?"

"Oh, yes—he still flies up against the screen, but when I try to shoo him toward the door, he just crouches in a corner. And there's a spot on top of his head where the feathers are sort of ruffled, so I thought . . ."

She didn't finish the terrible thought.

"I'll come out," I decided. Potomac wasn't far—six miles at the most. I could get there and back in time for class, and free us both from the worry of an injured bird.

Betty, sounding enormously relieved, gave me the address and directions to Firethorn Court.

"You'll recognize the house by the sheets," she said.

"Sheets?"

"Oh, I guess I didn't tell you. I was afraid he'd hurt himself flying against the screen, so I covered the porch with sheets to darken it—except at the door, so he could find his way out."

I recognized the house from a block away—a staid and spacious white-brick colonial on a street lined with equally staid and spacious homes. I wondered what the neighbors thought of the gaily festooned Conner home.

The screened porch was sizable, occupying an entire wing of the house, and it was hung on all three sides with a random assortment of sheets—florals, stripes, plaids, and solids in decorator colors, rippling gently in the morning breeze. In front of this masterpiece stood Betty, a smallish, energetic woman who must have devoted the better part of an afternoon to this project, climbing a ladder to hang the sheets in place with drapery hooks, overlapping them carefully, and then anchoring them with rocks at the bottom. It was an ambitious undertaking, even for a very determined woman.

Betty had no regret about depleting her linen closet for the cause. Her only regret was that it hadn't worked. The hawk, enclosed in this colorful bower, had continued to ignore the escape route at the end where the door was left invitingly open. He stayed huddled in a dim corner of the porch.

"Isn't he a beauty?" Betty breathed.

He was, indeed, a beautiful bird, an adult red-shouldered hawk, and he appeared to be in prime condition except for that small patch of ruffled feathers on his crown.

I approached him gradually, talking quietly. He didn't cringe when I stroked the top of his head, but he made a strange unhawk-like sound down in his throat. His fierce golden eyes were bright and alert. They focused on the index finger I raised and followed it intently as I moved it back and forth, up and down. He certainly didn't seem like a brain-damaged creature.

But I am not an expert on hawk care, and I thought it best, after his episode of trauma and fasting, to get him into expert hands.

Betty produced a large, clean carton (lined with a towel for comfort), and with gloved hands I picked up the docile bird. He did not struggle. He snuggled against my jacket, then shyly buried his head beneath the crook of my arm.

I held him for a minute before lowering him into the carton. It was the first time I had ever held a hawk; I suspected, as I looked down at his magnificent feathering, that this was a first experience for him, too. I could not have been more awed than I was.

Betty looked on, wide-eyed.

"Do you know," she said, "most people couldn't care less what happens to a hawk. My neighbor wouldn't even cross the street to look at it. I was so excited over this beautiful bird on my porch that I wanted to share it with someone. So I called her. Do you know what she said? She said, 'What do I want to see a hawk for?'"

We carried the box into the house and Betty made coffee while I telephoned Jane Zuke, certified rehabilitator of hawks, and arranged to deliver the patient to her.

With the carton on the seat beside me, I checked the dashboard clock. My exercise class was just getting started, six miles away, and I was just getting started on a 20-mile trip in the opposite direction.

When I pulled out of Jane Zuke's driveway an hour later, class was all over—but I was assured that Betty's hawk was in capable, caring hands.

On preliminary examination, Jane found nothing seriously wrong, nothing to suggest internal injuries or a fatal disease. She noted that the bird was alert and his eyes focused well. He was thin—probably just hungry and dehydrated. A diet of mice, she thought, would restore him in a couple of days. She promised a progress report.

As good as her word, she called the next day and I relayed the good news to Betty, who was busy washing the sheets that had enclosed her porch. She was happy to know that the patient was eating well and gaining strength.

Two more days passed and another call—an alarming call— came from Betty. From her strained voice I knew at once that something was wrong. Bad news from Jane Zuke about the hawk? I listened apprehensively.

"That hawk," Betty said, almost choking in her distress. "It was there on the porch for *two days* before I knew about it!"

The story came out haltingly. Betty had a twice-a-week maid who hadn't been in the States long and didn't speak much English.

"When she came to work this morning," Betty reported, "she looked out on the porch and said, 'Where is your bird?' And then I found out she'd seen it there *last Monday*. It was sitting right there on the table—and she didn't even mention it!"

"And you found it on Wednesday," I remembered.

"That's right." Anger and distress mingled in her voice, and I could well imagine her tone when she asked Lucia, "Why didn't you tell me?"

"She knows I love birds," Betty said. "I'd told her I was thinking of getting a parakeet."

I began to get the picture. "And she thought . . ."

"Can you believe it? She said, 'I think you get your parakeet.'"

Lucia, I remarked, must have thought parakeets come in extra-large sizes in the States.

But Betty, still agonizing for the captive that had spent two days and nights under her roof without food or drink, could see no humor in the mistake.

I don't think she was able to forgive Lucia, much less appreciate the comedy of the error, until word came from Jane Zuke, later in the week, that the hawk had been released in hospitable habitat.

He was strong and confident in flight, Jane reported, showing no sign of ill effects from his traumatic experience.

"Fully recovered," she said. And with those magic words, Betty could shake off the nightmare that had haunted her and think instead of the beauty of her hawk, flying free.

THE TOP-SECRET FALCON

"Bird call," read the note on the table. "Anon. He'll call back."

Anonymous calls aren't unusual in this household. There's nothing mysterious about them. Most of them are just carelessly anonymous, from people who are so intent on learning the identity of a strange bird that they neglect to identify themselves. But this one was very carefully anonymous, as Ted explained when I asked for an elaboration of his cryptic note.

"A youngish fellow," he guessed. "He wouldn't give his name or phone number. He sounded vague and sort of cagey. He wants to know something about hawks in the Blue Ridge Mountains."

That sounded like a question Ted could have answered just as well as I, but he confessed that he couldn't quite figure out what information was wanted.

"He'll call you. He sounds very intense."

Intense was the word for the mystery man. When he reached me, he began with the urgent statement, "I need to know about hawks in the Blue Ridge."

He didn't say why he "needed" this information, or precisely what he needed to know.

"Just what is your question?" I asked, feeling that he was concealing his real purpose.

He wanted to know, first, if there are red-tailed hawks in that area, and upon getting an affirmative answer, whether they get their full color before they achieve their full size.

He seemed disconcerted to learn that immature red-tailed hawks are fully grown before they get their distinctive red tail feathers.

The conversation was getting nowhere. The young man, for some reason, wasn't leveling with me. Impatient with subterfuge, I said, "If you'll tell me what it is you want to know and why, I'll try to help."

There was a long pause while he struggled (for words? for confidence?), and then the story came tumbling out, in that earnest voice.

"You see, I found this hawk trapped on the screened porch at my father's house down the road." Screened porches are hazardous to hawks, I thought, remembering Betty Conner's experience.

"I don't know how long it had been there—maybe a week or more. The family was away and the house was empty. I want to know what kind of hawk it is. "

Just a simple ID call, after all. Why the mystery?

"It has a red tail," he reported, "but it's small—about the size of a blue jay. The tail isn't all red. It has a dark band and a white band at the end."

I thought at once about the lovely, colorful American kestrel, often called the sparrow hawk, with its russet tail. When I asked for more details to confirm my guess, he said promptly, "Just a minute. I'll get him and see."

With the bird in hand, he gave a feather-by-feather, guidebook description of the kestrel: rusty back, bluish wings, a round head and short beak ("like a parakeet"), white cheeks, and black "whisker marks."

I made the natural assumption that the bird, having been without food for so long, was dead, but when I remarked on the state of "the body," the young man exclaimed, "Oh, no! He's alive! He's sitting right here on my wrist while I'm talking to you."

The pride in his voice was justifiable. Kestrels just aren't very approachable birds. But the young man claimed he'd had the captive eating from his hand in a couple of days.

"He was kind of peaked when I found him," he confided. "I think he may have found a mouse or two on the porch—they keep the dog food out there—but he had to be pretty empty. I gave him some hamburger—the only thing I had in my refrigerator—and that just went right through him. So I went out and caught a lizard. He knew exactly what to do with that."

All the caginess was gone. Words came pouring out. He had a natural eagerness to share this marvelous experience and to learn all he could about his house guest.

"Is this the same as a sparrow hawk?" he asked. "Do they eat sparrows?"

"Sparrow hawk," I told him, is really an inappropriate name for this small falcon, who is more likely to feed on grasshoppers, dragonflies, and small rodents than on small birds. That was important, relevant information—and it led to a confidential, half-shy revelation—the real underlying reason for the call.

"You see, I want to keep him and train him—so I have to know what to feed him and all that."

There was the matter of law, I cautioned. The Migratory Bird Treaty Act prohibits the possession of any wild migratory bird except by persons who have special permits.

"I know that," he said quickly. "I'm going to ask the state game warden about getting a permit. But before I could do that, I'd have to know the name of the bird."

So that was why he was being so secretive. He was afraid to give his name for fear of being reported for illegal possession of a wild bird.

Convinced of his good faith, I read him a complete diet list for kestrels from a reference book at hand and suggested that he get in touch with the local Raptor Society for further guidance on feeding and possibly on falconry—a subject on which I choose to remain ignorant, being inherently opposed to keeping birds in captivity. But despite that bias, I had to acknowledge that this kestrel was in sympathetic hands, hands that had saved it from starvation.

I expressed amazement at how quickly he had tamed a notoriously skittish bird and told him how many times my photographer husband had been frustrated in his efforts to get close enough to a kestrel to get a picture. At that, my anonymous caller dropped his guard completely.

"He can get a picture of this one," he boasted, "right here in my living room."

He readily gave me his name, address, and directions to his home, some 50 miles out in Virginia.

It was worth the drive on the following weekend to see the handsome kestrel, comfortably at home in the Welch living room. Delbert, the proud host, was only too happy to pose for pictures with the bird he hoped to adopt legally.

He had already gone to great lengths to create a hospitable environment. He had brought in a dead sapling and anchored it in a tub of rocks by the fireplace to create suitable perches for the kestrel. But the bird was equally comfortable perching on a potted plant, on the chain of a hanging lamp, or on Delbert's gloved wrist.

"I really want to keep this fellow," Delbert said earnestly. "And I think he takes to me."

So it seemed. There was a natural rapport between bird and man.

Not relying solely on his own good instincts, Delbert had studied all available sources at the library to prepare him for his responsibilities, in anticipation of getting the proper permit, and had laid in a supply of mice to keep his guest happy.

"Where did you get them?" Ted asked curiously.

Delbert grinned, half embarrassed. "At the pet store. I buy 'em by the dozen. He likes 'em live."

The kestrel, well-fed on prime quality white mice, flew to a high perch on his make-believe tree and gazed down serenely at the two dogs on the rug, who understood perfectly their master's stern instructions to leave the bird alone. We left, convinced that Delbert Welch could tame and train almost any animal.

"There are a lot of these birds around here," he told us, walking us to the car. "You can see them feeding out over the field right

125

across the road." He was clearly delighted over this new discovery of a bird he had never noticed before.

We sent Delbert copies of the pictures Ted had taken, and he called to thank us. We were, by now, old friends.

"Did you get your permit?" I asked, hoping for his sake that he had in spite of my ingrained prejudice.

"Naw," Gilbert said, and I could visualize his sheepish half-grin of self-amusement. "I let him go. He's out there, flying over that field with the rest of 'em. It's better that way."

I thought so, too.

"But I'll bet," the young man added, "that if I went out there and called him and held out my hand, he'd come and land on my wrist."

I wouldn't be at all surprised.

❖

A QUESTION OF AGE

Idle curiosity prompts many of the questions that come my way. A person who knows nothing of the natural history of birds may see a flock of Canada geese in migration and wonder, "Where did they come from? Where are they going?" Another, viewing the same scene, may think in terms of statistical specifics: "How fast can they fly? How far do they fly in a day? How many of them migrate each season?"

All of these are common questions. But one of the most common has to do with longevity. "What is the average life span of the common crow? I was just wondering . . ."

It's not the kind of question I expected to be answering when I volunteered to be a bird identifier. Not being statistically oriented, I'm especially grateful to those who are. Thanks to thousands of bird-banders (most of whom are volunteers), we have a wealth of statistics that offer insights into the life style and life span of many species. I find many intriguing statistics in John K. Terres' *The Audubon Society Encyclopedia of North American Birds*. Flipping the pages of this eight-pound tome, I can quickly come up with the answer: "Records indicate that six to eight years is average for a crow. In captivity they have been known to survive to be 20 years or more."

I turned to Terres one day when a man called to ask the average life span of a blue jay. Off the top of my head, I guessed about eight or nine years, but I wanted to be accurate even if I was only satisfying idle curiosity. Looking under the crow family for blue jays, I read out the information: ". . . many records of banded blue jays living to 6-9 years; several 10 years; one 11 years, 6 months; one . . . banded wild bird to 15 years."

The caller thanked me and explained that he was not motivated by mere curiosity. His sister-in-law, he said, had recently lost a pet blue jay that she had for 18 years, and was inconsolable in her grief. It was not only that she had lost a long-time companion, a vital part of her daily life, but that she had failed in her responsibility—that the bird's death was somehow her fault.

"But 18 years is phenomenal for a blue jay," I said. "Probably twice as long as it would have lived as a wild bird."

"I'm sure she'll be glad to hear that," he said.

I offered to call his sister-in-law, to console her if I could with assurances that she had kept the jay alive far beyond its normal life expectancy. Secondly, I wanted to verify the bird's age. Was it really 18 years old?

"Eighteen and a half," said Lucy Liu, when I telephoned her home in New Jersey.

Like anyone recently bereft of a family member, she was eager to talk, to relate not just vital statistics but incidents that made this bird-personality unique and beloved. I listened with the feeling that I had unexpectedly stepped into the role of grief therapist.

She recalled very well the spring day in 1969 when she had rescued two baby jays that had fallen from their nest. They were no larger than a hen's egg, she said, and had no feathers, so they were surely only a few days old. She undertook round-the-clock feedings and nursing care, making the small hatchlings the focus of the household routine.

After a month she was able to release one of the pair to the mother's custody (she was sure it was the mother, not the father, who waited patiently in the home tree). The other baby did not do so well. It had an injured leg and had to be kept under constant surveillance.

Apologizing unnecessarily for her halting English, Lucy Liu went on to relate how she had tried to teach the young bird survival skills, but in spite of all her efforts, it never learned to catch flies and it could fly only a few feet—not far enough or fast enough to elude all the potential predators in the outside world.

She did try, once, when her charge was two months old, to turn it over to the mother, but she met with a classic scene of parental rejection. The adult bird screamed at her own offspring, then turned her back on it. In all likelihood, she was preoccupied by that time with a second brood. In any case, she made it clear that this youngster was no longer her problem.

So it became Lucy's problem. She got a large cage and set out to make a comfortable home for the abandoned infant. She put the cage in the bathroom at night, but the bird cried so long and so loudly that she concluded it must be lonely. When she moved it into her bedroom the crying stopped. It seemed natural to call the bird "Baby."

"I didn't think it would ever live to be an adult," she said.

Lucy nursed the bird through childhood illnesses, giving it vitamins and minerals, and for colds, acromycin she got from her veterinarian. She became adept at interpreting symptoms and administering medicine. She was still calling the bird Baby when it developed arthritis at the advanced age of 16. By that time, she had known the rewards as well as the trials of parenthood, for Baby had become a good companion to the lone woman who had saved his life. He understood her language and talked back in a language all his own. If she scolded, he hung his head in sadness.

"He loved to please me, to obey me," she said, "and he took even bitter medicine from my finger." He showed affection and even played games, hiding peanuts for her to find.

"Their emotional aspect is very important," she told me. She knew from previous efforts to raise injured birds that it is not an easy thing to do. "God gives mother birds wisdom to raise their tiny, delicate babies which human beings could hardly achieve."

She tried to find that wisdom to care for Baby.

It would be hard to imagine more tender, loving care. She kept a heating pad in his cage at night, and he would settle down in a warm spot for his sleep in a quiet, darkened room. After he was ten or eleven years old, he began to sleep later and to take daytime naps as well. She increased the room temperature to 80 degrees to make sure he was comfortable.

As for diet, few birds enjoy such gourmet fare and variety. It was not enough for Lucy Liu to offer fresh food and water (changed four times a day and served in meticulously clean containers). She cooked most of his food, "except for clean fresh fruits and vegetables," and even washed and baked his bird-seed ("to avoid heavy chemicals or mold"). Baby dined on diced lean beef, chopped liver, egg yolk and a little egg white; foods rich in vitamin B, such as wheat germ; fresh corn and carrots; and fruit for dessert, although she had to limit his intake of fruits and fresh green peas because too much of either caused diarrhea.

And in the end, she had failed him. Of that she was convinced, and nothing I said could persuade her otherwise. The veterinarian who had prescribed for Baby's arthritis had said many of the same things I was saying, but she had rejected his explanation that the bird simply died of old age.

Baby died, she insisted, for lack of proper medication.

"He could have lived five or six years more," Lucy asserted confidently. "He was in good condition except for the arthritis. He was very strong. But he had diarrhea when I took him to his doctor. It had to be from bacteria. It was the bacteria that killed him—and I should have known."

She did not blame the veterinarian for any error in treatment. She blamed herself for not giving Baby the medication he needed to fight off the bacteria that cut his life short at the age of eighteen and a half.

"I am responsible," she said, with fierce, insistent logic. "I will tell you why. No one could know Baby as well as I knew him."

About that, at least, there could be no question.

THE NUMBERS GAME

Long before the first frost, the telephone is kept busy with migration questions. To many people, migration means waterfowl, and waterfowl means Blackwater, the national wildlife refuge on Chesapeake Bay that a birder friend calls "the Serengeti of the Eastern Shore."

Day after day I answer the question, "When is the best time to go to Blackwater?"

A friend, just back from his annual pilgrimage, had his own answer. "I like to go early," he said, "before there are too many birds. I like to study the small flocks, where you have a chance to observe individuals. When they start coming in the thousands, they all look alike. I get dizzy watching them."

I knew the feeling. I had experienced it with Canada geese, years ago when Ted and I were novice birders.

We had heard of Blackwater, where geese were supposed to gather by the thousands to spend the winter. "You have to go to Blackwater," one of the old hands told us. "You've never seen anything like it."

We did not need Canada geese for our life-list. In our younger days, we had seen plenty of them along the Mississippi Flyway. We had heard their haunting cries, like the distant barking of dogs, when they flew over at night, and it was not uncommon to see a flock as large as 200 passing over by daylight. But numbers into the thousands were inconceivable. Yes, we would definitely have to go to Blackwater.

Prudently, I telephoned in advance to make sure we were not wasting a two-hour trip. The eager young naturalist who answered the phone was polite enough not to betray amusement at my naive question, "Do you have any geese there?" But there was a significant pause before he answered with a question of his own: "How many trips do you plan to make over here this fall?"

I wasn't sure. We had never been there before, but if we liked it, we might come back. "It depends . . ."

He got the picture.

"I just wanted to say," he explained helpfully, "that if you're making only one trip, it would be better to wait until Thanksgiving weekend. We'll have 130,000 by then. Right now, we have only 85,000."

He actually said that. *Only 85,000 geese.* Did he imagine I could tell the difference between 85,000 and 130,000? Did he really think I would miss the 45,000 that had not yet arrived from the far north?

Encouragingly, he assured me that more were coming in every day—mostly Canadas, plus a few scattered flocks of snow geese. The swans would come later.

"Get an early start," he advised. "It's best to be here before nine o'clock if you can."

We were there before eight o'clock on a brisk October morning with a tinge of frost in the air and the glow of golden leaves substituting for sunlight. We had begun to see high-flying flocks of geese as soon as we crossed the Bay Bridge—long, slender chains of them, not in the classic V-formation, but in wavy lines. By the time we reached Cambridge, we had stopped pointing and shouting, "There's another! There's another!" In one hour, I had seen more geese than I had seen throughout my entire life—and we were not even within sight of the refuge.

Suddenly it occurred to me: "That 85,000 he was talking about—that's just on the refuge itself. Obviously, they don't all land on the refuge!"

Obviously. Driving through farmlands, we passed field after field that seemed to be planted in Canada geese, their necks extending like thick black stems rising out of the grass or stubble. There were blinds in those fields, too, reminders that hunting is big business on the Eastern Shore.

We stopped the car and opened the windows to observe the geese more closely as they browsed and gabbled among themselves. Understandably wary, they edged away from the car, but made no effort to fly. After a 3000-mile journey, they were not eager to be airborne again without due cause.

Driving on slowly, we became aware of the increasing din around us. The flocks in the air were dropping lower and lower, honking excitedly as they changed to V-shapes, then broke apart for the final gliding descent with landing gears lowered and wings set as brakes.

The target was a stubblefield on our left, already crowded with earlier arrivals gleaning grains of corn left from the harvest. They shifted and regrouped, making a greater commotion as the newcomers joined them. How could there be room for them all in that one field?

They wouldn't stay there, of course. This was only a way station, a place to rest and feed. Tomorrow a new wave of migrants would come in to displace those who would move on to final destinations along the coast as far as North Carolina.

We stood unnoticed at the edge of the cornfield, in the midst of the paratroop invasion. Above us, all around us, were strings of geese in all directions, from horizon to horizon. Their honking filled our ears like stereophonic music coming through earphones, excluding all other sounds, all other consciousness, creating the sensation of sound being produced inside the head.

Binoculars hung around our necks unused. We were at close enough range to see every detail of the brown bodies, the black heads with their white chin-straps, the semicircles of white that showed on their tails as the great birds came in for a landing.

We tried to count. How many on the ground? How many in the air? Ignorant of the techniques for estimating flocks, we gave up, completely overwhelmed by numbers that had to be in the tens of thousands.

When we reached it, Blackwater Refuge was almost an

anticlimax. Geese browsed in the fields and congregated in the impoundments. Geese waddled confidently across the road, blocking traffic. Geese dropped out of the sky in squadrons.

It was almost a relief to find that there were ducks, too—mallards, black ducks, pintails, and widgeons, looking ridiculously small by comparison. Far out in the main impoundment we spotted a flock of some 50 snow geese, sparkling white except for their black wing-tips. But the Canadas dominated.

Noisy and busy as they were, there was a settled air about them, as if they had reached the end of the line and were content with their winter quarters. Apparently the food crop here was ample, even if their numbers continued to grow at the same staggering rate.

At nine o'clock, I would have guessed there were as many geese *over* the refuge as *on* the refuge—and still they kept coming. By ten o'clock, the air traffic had diminished considerably; by eleven, there were only a few stragglers. Then we understood why the naturalist had advised us to arrive early. The big show was all over for the day.

Of course, we would come back. We would come back in November to see the tundra swans, to watch snow geese in flight, and to scan the flocks for the less common blue phase of the snow geese—but not for the sake of counting the promised 130,000 Canadas that were due by Thanksgiving. We had already seen more than we could absorb.

Seeing is not believing. We could not begin to grasp the magnitude of the migration—not even the small segment of it we had actually witnessed in a brief four-hour span.

Exhausted, as if we had made the long flight from Alaska ourselves, we settled down in a quiet place for lunch. The background babble of the geese simmered down to a murmur. The sun had come out and the sky was empty of birds, except for the after-images produced when we closed our overworked eyes.

Then we heard a loud honking nearby. Circling above us was one lone goose, lost and calling frantically for his relatives. Automatically, we raised our binoculars—as if this were the first bird we had seen all day. As we followed him in his desperate quest, we were at last able to grasp the drive and the drama and the essential ordeal of the migration.

shafer

✛

WINTER CALLERS

Daylight hours are unbearably short. There are so many places to go, so many fleeting wonders to see in these brief hours. It's a cardinal sin to miss the hordes of waterfowl that gather along the Potomac and Chesapeake Bay, the blizzards of snow geese, the dazzling white tundra swans, the familiar Canada geese in tens of thousands. We have seen it all before, and yet we are impelled to make pilgrimages each year to pay our respects, to make sure this marvel has not disappeared from the earth. We need to see the regal canvasbacks afloat on the Choptank River, to search for harlequins and eider along the frigid coast, to find the lovely purple sandpipers hopping over the wave-washed rocks of the jetties.

We need more time to prowl the woods. This is the time for saw-whet and long-eared owls, for winter wrens and hermit thrushes. It is a time for rough-legged hawks and harriers over the fields. It is time, too, to keep the feeders and the birdbath filled and to enjoy the quiet pleasures of indoor birdwatching and lazy reading by the fire, interrupted by reports from the outside world.

The telephone rings . . .

✥

THE UGLY VULTURE

The day of the first snow brought early reports of traffic snarls, Washington-style, and school closings. But the offices of the Audubon Naturalist Society were open on schedule, and the receptionist had taken a call from a woman in my general neighborhood who had seen a "huge, mean-looking bird with a red head" sitting on a fence post near her house. Would I investigate it?

The bird that immediately came to mind was the turkey vulture. He is "huge" by almost any standards, with a two-yard wing-span; he has a red head; and since he is not exactly a pretty bird, I suppose he could appear mean-looking to anyone with a lively imagination. I decided to call the woman before going to the extreme of shoveling my car out of the driveway to go on a wild-bird chase.

Her further description confirmed my first guess. But it was not identification she wanted, it was reassurance. She cared not about the bird's name, but about his intentions.

He was still sitting there on the post, within sight of her front door, and she was afraid to let either her children or her dog out in the face of that menacing presence. Would he attack them? And if not, why was he sitting there in the snow?

It was undoubtedly because of the snow that the bird was grounded, although why it chose that particular fence post I couldn't say. Certainly not for the sake of preying on dogs and children, I explained, because turkey vultures (commonly called buzzards in some parts of the country) feed only on dead carcasses.

That didn't make matters much better. Her revulsion was as strong as her original fear. She didn't want to *think* about a bird with such repulsive eating habits, much less look at him from her front window. Her attitude modified somewhat when I pointed out the beneficial sanitation service vultures perform by clearing our landscape and highways of rotting flesh, and the considerable tax savings it affords us to have these highly efficient garbage collectors working for us free of charge, 365 days a year, with no annual leave.

I based my defense of the unappreciated vulture on purely utilitarian values. Any mention of aesthetic appeal would be wasted on anyone who has not seen him in flight. That appeal is missing in the sitting turkey vulture. He is floppy and untidy. His feathers are a dull black, not glistening like those of the well-groomed crow. And his red head has no resemblance to that of the red-headed woodpecker, for example, because it is the dull red of rough, unfeathered skin. Unlike the bald eagle and the baldpate duck (American widgeon) that derive their names from the *appearance* of baldness produced by white feathers on their heads, the turkey vulture is truly bald. This is a matter of good design, enabling him to probe into carcasses without fouling his feathers. But at close range it is difficult to see any beauty in the folds of red skin.

This detail is not noticeable, however, when the bird is aloft. In flight he is a most magnificent bird, soaring with a grace and ease that inspires envy in the earthbound. He lifts off his perch with slow, heavy flaps, but once he is airborne, he circles and glides with no effort at all, riding the thermal currents as if they were made for him, tilting his wing-tips upward to form the familiar dihedral pattern that makes him distinctive in flight. Watching him as he circles over the highway, it's hard to remember that he is at work up there, constantly scanning as he sails, ready to drop down and remove the carnage of wildlife that we leave behind us on the road.

Turkey vultures and their close relatives, the smaller black vultures, are seen from city streets as well as interstate highways. When I was working in Washington, my homeward route took me along the edge of Rock Creek Park, where flocks of vultures have been roosting for 150 years. I looked forward to the curve in the road that opened up a view of the sunset and the dark silhouettes of the great birds circling toward the zoo for their night's rest. For a time, these same vultures developed the habit of perching on the roof of the venerable Kennedy-Warren building, and the elderly residents of that Connecticut Avenue apartment who enjoyed watching the birds in flight saw nothing sinister or macabre about their presence.

There was at one time another vulture roost in Washington, on the far side of the Georgetown Reservoir on MacArthur Boulevard. On a clear, crisp winter day we stopped alongside the reservoir to scan its surface for ducks while we listened to Beethoven's Sixth Symphony on the car radio. Our attention was drawn to a flock of some 30 vultures circling over the reservoir. Soaring, wheeling, gliding in graceful patterns against the backdrop of a brilliant blue sky, they seemed to catch the spirit of the music in their movements. It was like watching a great outdoor ballet, spontaneous and unrehearsed but executed with artistic perfection. We could almost convince ourselves that these birds were equipped with listening devices of their own, tuned to the same music we were hearing, and that they were reacting to it in a way we could not.

Sight and sound blended so perfectly that the two became inseparable in memory. Now, whenever we hear the familiar musical theme, we recall that inspired performance; and when we see a flock of vultures in synchronized flight, we think of the music of Beethoven's Sixth.

"HOW BIG IN RELATION TO A MOCKINGBIRD?"

Six inches of snow had fallen over Melody Lane, and the thick, furry flakes were still coming down steadily. In the silence that accompanies a heavy snowfall, the telephone rang, disturbing the illusion of isolation. There was word from the invisible outside world.

Someone had a rare bird he wanted identified. He was a college student, a stranger in the area, house-sitting for his brother in Alexandria. He did not know birds, he admitted, but he had been watching one in the back yard for some time and trying to match it with pictures in his brother's bird guide. After some study, he had concluded that it had to be a Clark's nutcracker.

Was this possible?

Anything was possible in a crazy winter that had brought a boreal chickadee to Baltimore, a northern shrike to Sandy Point, a western tanager to Takoma Park, and flocks of common redpolls to our own back yard. It was unlikely that a Clark's nutcracker would have wandered so far from its Rocky Mountain habitat, but who was I to say it was impossible?

Still, long experience with futile chases based on telephone descriptions prompted caution. It had been less than a month since I had traveled some 20 miles to see a "rare" bird that turned out to be a song sparrow. So I asked myself what the commonest bird was that could conceivably be mistaken for a Clark's nutcracker by an inexperienced observer.

"How big is it," I asked, "in relation to a mockingbird?" The question was carefully worded to establish the caller's background without insulting his intelligence.

"I don't know your mockingbird," he replied. "We don't have

them in our part of the country. But in relation to a blue jay, it's much larger. It's more the size of a small crow."

That would make it considerably larger than a mockingbird, and I began to take interest. Under further questioning, the young man described the bird as large and gray, with a heavy beak, black wing-tips, and a loud, raucous voice.

That sounded right. And the clincher came with the observation that the bird was sitting in a pine tree, tearing a pine cone apart. This was definitely not mockingbird behavior.

Still skeptical, I admitted it was worth a firsthand look. But not by me. Not if it meant a 30-mile trip around the Beltway in heavy snow and 30 miles back during rush hour. But there were only two hours of daylight left, and the bird could be gone tomorrow. I took down the address and directions, and said I'd try to find a Virginia birder who was willing to undertake the mission.

It's the kind of challenge that birders will respond to in the worst of weather. I called Owen Fang, who was within five miles of the described location. Frustrated that he wasn't free to go, he agreed to send a trusted surrogate and asked for detailed directions.

"It's at the top of a hill," I warned him, "and the road hasn't been cleared. The only safe way to get there is on foot."

"I'll call David Abbott," Owen said. "He's young and healthy; he won't mind the hike."

It was dark before the phone rang again. Snow was still falling. The streetlights had been turned on.

This could be word of a real find—a Virginia record for the Clark's nutcracker. I almost regretted that I hadn't made the discovery myself.

"This is the Fang Bird Identification Service." Owen's dry tone prepared me for the report that followed. "It was a mockingbird."

A mockingbird. For that, David Abbott—young and healthy— had hiked three-quarters of a mile uphill through heavy snow. That was bad enough, but the return trip without the glow of anticipation was far worse, even though it was downhill all the way.

Deeply chagrined, I asked that my apologies be relayed to David.

"He didn't mind," Owen assured me. "He doesn't blame you. You just got a lousy description."

We reviewed the description and agreed it was accurate in at least two respects: It was a gray bird with black wing tips, and it could be very noisy, even raucous. The rest of it was a blend of imagination and poor perception.

"The thing that gets me," said Owen, "is the remark that the bird had a pine cone in his beak. That just doesn't sound like a mockingbird. But do you know what? Look in the field guide and you'll see that's the way the Clark's nutcracker is pictured. That young fellow did what a lot of amateurs do: He looked at the picture first, then made his description fit the bird in the picture."

The next morning I was called in from snow-shoveling by the insistent ring of the telephone. An excited woman was calling to announce that she had seen an ivory-billed woodpecker in her woods, out in Fairfax County, Virginia. She knew the species was supposed to be extinct, but she was absolutely certain of her identification. There simply could be no question about it. She couldn't understand why I wasn't eager to rush right out and look for it.

I went back to shoveling snow.

✣

REAL HAWKS
DON'T EAT STRUDEL

A young voice piped in my ear—a very young voice, as high and clear as a chickadee's spring song. Whether male or female, I couldn't say. The name, Min Thua, gave no clue. But gender was not important.

What *was* important was that Min Thua had just spotted a strange bird in a backyard tree and was sufficiently curious and enterprising to call the Audubon Society for help in identifying it.

Min Thua was a good observer with a passion for detail and, although lacking the basic birder's vocabulary, gave enough information to identify the visitor as a red-tailed hawk, a very impressive raptor. No wonder Min Thua sounded excited.

"Is this rare?"

I hesitated. "Rare" is a relative term, dependent on the season and the location. Red-tailed hawks are common enough in this area, but they're certainly not common in the average back yard.

"Where do you live?" I asked.

"Bethesda, Maryland," Min Thua replied, so promptly that I almost expected this information to be followed by a zip code.

I, too, live in Bethesda, Maryland, and on comparing addresses, we learned that there is only a mile or two between us, as the hawk flies. This was of special interest to me because we, too, have been visited by a red-tailed hawk on a fairly regular basis this winter.

The crows first called our attention to it. A boisterous gang of four, they were out looking for mischief when they spotted the chunky hawk sitting stolidly in a big oak within view of our breakfast table. The game began—a favorite game with crows known (to us, if not to them) as "mobbing." Emitting the special call they reserve for announcing the discovery of a hawk, which serves as an invitation to all crows within earshot to join in the game, they took turns swooping down on their victim. With harsh cries and flapping wings, they tormented him until he was forced to forsake his comfortable perch and fly off through the trees.

More crows appeared, zeroing in on the target from all directions, and the chase continued all through our breakfast hour.

That chase scene became an almost daily event. We fell into the habit of scanning the tree skeletons across the way for the silhouette of the hawk against the early morning sky. Often we found him on his favorite perch, silent and immobile, with no crows to disturb him. Sometimes we didn't see him until the game was underway and the taunting crows were sailing after him, circling in front of our window, disappearing over the roof, and reappearing against the backdrop of woods across the lane.

Given the tenacity of the crows, it would not be surprising if the chase led them as far as Min Thua's house.

I asked about crows, but Min Thua had not seen any. The hawk was just sitting quietly all by itself, not eating, not doing anything.

Our hawk—if I can lay claim to it—gets around.

A few days earlier, a neighbor only a couple of blocks away had called to report that a hawk was sitting in a tree in her yard, eating a squirrel. She offered ringside seats at her window, but I was on my way to an appointment so it was Ted who had the opportunity of watching the diner attack his meal efficiently and with relish. We had no doubt that this was our hawk.

It was reassuring to know that the hawk had squirrel on his menu. I had often wondered how he fared, hunting in our neighborhood, and in fact I had been concerned that he might prey on the birds at our feeder if he didn't find enough rodents about to satisfy his needs. Though we often see mice and small voles in the garden, we rarely spot a mouse or a rat. But squirrels have been overabundant in recent years, and overly inventive in robbing our feeders—even stealing suet to round out their diet of pilfered sunflower seed. So it seems only fair that a red-tailed hawk should appear to restore nature's balance.

Our hawk was missing for a few days following Min Thua's call. I pictured him basking in a crow-less back yard and wondered if he had relocated permanently.

Then, on a drizzly Sunday morning when a cold rain was washing away the gray remains of the last snow, a call came from a woman who had "a huge, chicken-like bird" sitting on the ground in her back yard. Her description was less precise than Min Thua's, but her "chicken-like bird" was unquestionably a red-tailed hawk.

"I've never seen such a thing before," she said. "What would it be doing here?"

"Looking for food, most likely," I said, and when I asked her to define "here," I learned that she was less than a mile away. She could very well be entertaining our hawk. And royally.

She had, she admitted with a half-embarrassed laugh, made a strudel that—well, "hadn't turned out so good." It had fruit and nuts in it, so she threw it into the yard, thinking it might at least be palatable to the birds.

I wanted to tell her that real hawks don't eat strudel. Fruit and nuts aren't on their preferred list. But strudel could very well attract rats, which in turn could attract a hawk. Should I warn her of the rat problem?

"And then," she added as an afterthought, "I had some chicken necks and gizzards I didn't want, so I threw those out, too."

She was likely to have a lively back yard. With crows in the neighborhood, the hawk wouldn't have it to himself for long.

Never having seen a hawk before, she naturally wondered if they were rare. I told her that we see them regularly in the area and in fact often have one visiting our property.

"What do you feed him?" she asked.

It had never occurred to me to feed him anything. It occurs to me now that we've been running a squirrel farm for him, fattening an endless supply with oily black sunflower seed.

Min Thua, intent on writing a story about the hawk, called again with more questions. Are red-tailed hawks endangered? Where do they nest? What do they eat? Here was a youngster who had made a new acquaintance and was eager to learn all about it.

We chatted a while and then I asked a question. I, too, wanted to know more about my new acquaintance.

"How old are you?" I asked, hoping this was not too personal.

"Seven and a half," said Min Thua, with characteristic precision and, it seemed to me, a touch of pride.

I didn't dare ask, "Boy or girl?" It really wasn't important, except that it's awkward to refer to a person, even mentally, without benefit of pronoun. All I needed to know was that Min Thua was exhibiting early symptoms of bird-addiction and had sought me out as an accomplice.

A girl, I decided, for no logical reason. But I was remembering a seven-year-old girl from another era who pestered patient grown-ups with endless questions about the birds she saw; who studied pictures in the Chester Reed pocket guide and wrote the names, with appropriate dates, in a little blue notebook, never dreaming that this was the beginning of a life-list that would grow into the hundreds.

There's much to be said for getting an early start.

THE LURE OF THE CHRISTMAS COUNT

It happens every year about this time, as predictable as carols on the radio and the jingle of Salvation Army bells on street corners.

It happens at least once, and in some years several times. The script varies but the message is the same.

The telephone rings and the sound of a hesitant, timid voice forewarns me that I'm about to hear the eternal December question. The voice may be masculine or feminine, young or not-so-young, and the question is likely to begin:

"Would you tell me honestly . . .?"

"Do you think I should . . .?"

"Do I know enough to . . .?"

"Could I be any help at all . . .?"

They've begun to think of the Christmas Bird Count. They are, by their own humble admission, "just beginners" or "not really good birders" who have felt the lure of this annual birding marathon but are shy about offering their services, fearful of exposing their ignorance or, worse, of getting in the way.

Newcomers in the ranks of birding seem to think that it requires a certain level of expertise, a graduate degree of some sort, to qualify for this annual event.

This is not true.

Veterans are always in demand, of course, but how will you ever become a veteran if you don't go through basic training? And what better time to enlist than now?

An extra pair of eyes and an extra pair of hands are always welcome on any team. Anyone who knows how to count and how to use binoculars knows enough to go on a Christmas Count.

It helps, of course, to know at least some of the birds in the area, and the more the better. But no one is required to pass a test in field identification. Even the most inexperienced can probably distinguish a duck from a sparrow. What kind of duck? What kind of sparrow? The finer points of identification can be left to the veterans on the team. The sharp-eyed novice who can simply point and yell "Bird!" may have the satisfaction of adding a species to the day's list that might otherwise have been missed.

Keen ears are an asset, too, and the ability to recognize the calls of a few familiar birds, for the goal is to count not just species but every individual bird. "Heard birds," which often outnumber those actually seen, swell the totals and give a more accurate assessment of the winter bird population.

The most modest and self-effacing aspirants who are eager to be helpful but afraid they might instead be an impediment are comforted to know that they also serve who only make marks on the tally sheet. Anyone willing to do the paperwork releases a veteran for more active duty.

My own apprenticeship as a tally-keeper, twenty-odd years ago, is still a vivid memory. I learned very quickly how difficult it is to cope simultaneously with binoculars, a clipboard, and a pencil—especially in the rain.

It was a cold, driving rain that numbed the fingers and soaked the tally sheet. Overhead and underfoot it was the worst kind of day for a count. Birds took cover and fell silent. The few that moved were fuzzy blurs seen through steamed-over binoculars spattered with raindrops. It was, as they said, a good day for ducks, but even the ducks on the river were dimly seen through the curtain of rain.

At one point, head down against the wind and clipboard tucked inside my raincoat, I slipped on a muddy slope and slid ignominiously to the bottom. Our leader, kindly and solicitous, helped me to my feet, refrained from laughing at my plight, and asked if I'd like to go home and get into dry clothes.

Absolutely not! Miserable as it was, I was determined to hang in there. I wanted to know firsthand what this fabled dawn-to-dark ordeal was really like. But it was more than curiosity that kept me going. There was a certain group spirit that had settled over us when we met like conspirators in the darkness before dawn, sharing last-minute sips from thermoses, speaking in hushed tones, and making wry jokes about the weather.

We met at that unholy hour, I learned, because that's the hour when owls are likely to call—and a hoot in the darkness, answered by another hoot across the river, proved the point. Even in the rain, owls call. Our leader impressed me enormously by identifying them as great horned owls.

Two marks on the tally sheet.

More marks were recorded as members of the team called out cardinals, white-throated sparrows, and Carolina wrens, giving their distinctive call-notes from the bushes long before daylight.

By noon, when the scattered members of our party gathered to share bag lunches and the morning's experiences, the rain-warped tally sheet showed too much white space for six hours of hard work. But the rain had stopped, and a brisk northwest wind was sweeping the gray from the sky. We scraped heavy clumps of mud from our boots and prepared to push on. Again, I was offered the beginner's option of dropping out, and again I declined. Quitting at half-time was unthinkable. With clear visibility and the chance of adding more birds to the list, I was eager to resume the count.

For once, I gave thanks that December days are short. The curtain of dusk fell none too soon to put an end to that exhausting day.

Then there was the warm reward of the Tally Rally, a kind of bonding experience for those who have stayed the course from dawn to dark. Fatigued but triumphant, the scattered teams gathered for hot cider, steaming bowls of chili, and a final accounting of their day's work.

Looking around at the weary troops, ranging from teenagers to venerable veterans, it occurred to me that this was only a small part of a great nation-wide endeavor—that this scene, like the opening of presents on Christmas morning, was being played out in different settings all over the country. I had just taken part in a great tradition that had been going on since 1900, and the little marks I had made on the tally sheet would be translated into figures published in a special issue of *American Birds*.

Next year . . . I was already looking ahead. Next year might bring ice and snow. Next year I would be a veteran.

"Do you think I should . . .?"

"Do I know enough . . .?"

"Could I be any help at all . . .?"

The answer is "Yes! Yes! Yes!" to all three questions. That first Christmas Count will be a day you'll never forget.

TWELFTH-NIGHT VISITORS

On the eve of Twelfth Night, the first pine siskins arrived at the thistle feeder, three darkly streaked little birds with bright yellow flashes on their wings. The next day a pair of Carolina wrens made their cheery appearance on the backyard scene, flitting from suet to sunflower seeds and staying companionably close together. The year had begun with good omens.

Twelfth Night has its traditions. For us it is the time of undecking the halls, putting away the tired trappings of the holidays, and writing reminders on next December's calendar, in firm resolve to be better organized another year. "Buy stamps." "Address Christmas cards." "Make wreath."

With a twelve-degree chill hanging over the snow-white landscape, it was a good day for indoor chores. I began dismantling the tree, still remarkably fresh and fragrant, keeping an eye on the feeder scene all the while. The wrens were cause for rejoicing. These perky little birds are year-round residents here on the northernmost frontier of their range, but a series of harsh winters has depleted the population. Not programmed to migrate, they have no impulse to escape a cold wave by moving farther south where food supplies are more accessible.

The two in the back yard were the first I had seen in several weeks. They came and went all through the morning, taking advantage of brief intervals when there were no house finches in sight, withdrawing discreetly when the quarreling finches returned to displace them. From time to time I pounded on the window to disperse the finches and give the wrens a turn, but the wrens and I were greatly outnumbered.

Some 50 miles away, a Mrs. Lott was having her problems with house finches, too, and in her exasperation she called the Audubon Naturalist Society for help. Her call was relayed to me.

What could she do to keep those greedy finches away without discouraging the "better birds?" I wish I knew.

There was a time when house finches were rare in the east. But these transplants from the West Coast have been all too successful here, even overwhelming house sparrows in our community. On the desirability scale, house finches rate higher than house sparrows; at least they're more colorful and they sing a pretty song. But they multiply just as rapidly, and we do object to subsidizing their burgeoning population with food intended for chickadees, titmice, cardinals, and goldfinches, which are all too often crowded out.

I commiserated with Mrs. Lott but could offer no practical suggestions. Then she asked if I had time for a little story she'd like to share. It was a wonderful Twelfth Night story, well worth retelling.

Mrs. Lott had finished "untrimming" her Christmas tree and left it standing in the living room, waiting for her husband to remove it. The only remaining holiday decoration was the evergreen wreath on the front door.

When her husband came in, a pair of Carolina wrens that had found warmth and shelter in the wreath flew out, straight past him and into the living room. One flew directly to the Christmas tree in the corner; the other perched on the mantle, no doubt the warmest perch it had found in many cold days.

Reluctantly, the Lotts opened the door and gently persuaded their little visitors to leave.

"I thought you'd like that little story," Mrs. Lott concluded.

Indeed I did. It was both intriguing and timely. I had been musing on the mysteries of our two little wrens, who seemed to disappear when bolder, more aggressive birds appeared at the feeder. Where did they hide? How did they know when the coast was clear? And how had they managed to survive when so many of their kind had perished?

Mrs. Lott's story inspired me to take a critical look at my own homemade evergreen wreath, still hanging on the door. It was far short of the ideal I had in mind, much too skimpy. Still, it was in a sheltered place and might conceivably provide a haven for a pair of clever wrens on a cold night. An unlikely possibility—but it would do no harm to leave it up for a few more days. Next year I could do better.

On my December calendar, I wrote a note: "Make a wreath—large and luxurious—wren-friendly."

❖

THE CALL OF THE WOODLAND LOON

"I've been hearing a loon," the caller began, after introducing herself.

I was about to express envy. The call of the loon is a sound I have never heard, except on records and television nature programs. I know local birders who have occasionally heard the haunting cry of a wintering loon on the Potomac not far from my home, but I have always missed it. I have missed it in Canada, too, and in Maine and the Adirondacks where loons nest. Somehow my timing has been wrong.

But before I could say, "Aren't you lucky?," the voice continued, "At least I think it's a loon. It's a shivery kind of call that sort of goes up the scale and trails off. It's hard to describe."

She had attempted to describe it to a friend who was familiar with loons, having heard them on his pond up in Maine. He was convinced that she was hearing a loon. But she was still a little uncertain, so she was seeking a second opinion.

I was dubious, knowing how hard it is to identify a bird positively on the basis of a verbal description of its voice. Still, it was possible she was near the river or a pond where a wintering loon might be calling from time to time.

The first order of business was to pinpoint the location.

She had heard the bird from her home in a new suburban development that was bordered by undisturbed woodland. I knew the area well and could not think of a body of water within a mile.

Neither could she.

"The sound came from the woods across the street," she said.

A loon in the woods? Highly unlikely, I told her. Loons haven't the knack for perching in trees.

"But couldn't it be migrating?" she persisted.

It was too early for the northward migration of loons. Moreover, the habitat was all wrong, lacking the one essential element: water. A loon out of water is a doomed bird. The unique anatomical structure that makes him a powerful swimmer and diver also makes him incapable of lifting off from terra firma. Even on water, he needs to paddle furiously for some distance before he can get his heavy body airborne. Stranded on dry land, he can only flop about awkwardly until a good Samaritan rescues him and restores him to a watery habitat.

All this was news to her, but she was prepared to believe that there was actually a loon in trouble deep in her woods. She had spent some time searching for it the first day, she said, but found nothing. And she didn't hear the call again until that night.

"You've heard it more than once, then?"

"Oh, yes. Every night this week. And last night it was quite close. I think it was in a tree right outside my window. It was eerie. But I couldn't see a thing."

A loon that calls from a tree at night has to be a loon spelled O-W-L.

The lady rejected this suggestion. "Oh, no. We have owls in the woods, too. I know owls when I hear them."

"What kind of owls do you have?" I asked.

"Oh, just the ordinary kind of hoot-owls, I guess. They say, 'Hoo-hoo-hoo-HOO.'" She had given a passable imitation of a barred owl.

"But there are owls with different voices," I explained. I was thinking of the quavery crescendo of the little screech owl. "Let me play a tape for you."

I set the cassette player close to the phone and started the owl tape. As soon as she heard the rise-and-fall notes of the screech owl, she shouted excitedly, "That's it! That's it!"

She was all ready to set out on an owl hunt.

I didn't want to discourage her, but I knew it would take

extraordinary luck and persistence to find the screech owl. Only eight inches in height, this is the smallest and probably the most elusive of owls that nest in our area. Strictly nocturnal, it simply disappears in the daytime, usually roosting in the dense cover of a conifer where it is very difficult to find.

I knew this from recent frustrating experience, having spent several days trudging up and down streets and invading back yards in our own suburban community, searching for a screech owl that was reported to me by a jogger who heard it regularly on his early-morning route. I gave up the quest when my informant advised me that the owl was no longer calling. Either it had moved on or, more likely, since winter is mating season for owls, it had found a mate and settled down to the business of nesting.

But I became convinced that screech owls are more common in urban and suburban woods than is generally supposed. They are not easily detected except by voice—and most people, like the lady with the woodland loon, don't recognize the voice when they hear it. I have never heard one in my immediate neighborhood, but finding one dead on the road less than a half-mile from home prompted speculation that there are many of them lurking unseen, possibly in our own woods.

While I was pondering the fate of the dead owl, a friend who lives only a mile away called with good news and bad. He reported, with some regret, that the pair of pileated woodpeckers had disappeared from his property. But the good news was that a pair of screech owls had taken over the cavity vacated by the woodpeckers and were making themselves quite at home.

I was quick to accept his invitation to come over and pay them a visit at dusk, the best time to see the owls flying. It's a rare treat to see a screech owl in action. With luck, I thought, I might even hear that quavery crescendo that had inspired an adventurous woman to go prowling through her woods in search of a loon.

✥

THE RETURN OF THE EAGLE

A bird hits the window with a sickening thud and falls to the ground. It may be dead, but more likely it is merely stunned and, after a few minutes of rest, it will revive and go on its way.

This rarely happens at our house, but I know from the number of telephone calls I get that it is a common occurrence. During the feeding season, I may have as many as three calls a day about window hits, with requests for identification of the bird and for emergency care instructions.

House finches, always abundant at local feeders, seem to be the most frequent victims. They gather in flocks at a feeder, and when alarmed they fly up in all directions without looking where they're going. If the feeder is close to a window (and the window is inexcusably clean and unobstructed), an occasional crash is inevitable.

Sometimes the bird remains stunned for some time and has to be rescued, especially in cold weather, when it should be brought indoors and kept warm and quiet in a cloth-lined shoebox for an hour or so until it's ready to fly again.

I'm prepared to give reassurance along with first-aid advice and the usual hint about putting the silhouette of a falcon on the window to prevent recurrences. But none of this was relevant when Mary Maichle called about a bird that had flown into her living room window.

Mary wanted to know what kind of bird it was, and from the way her voice was shaking I knew it couldn't be a house finch, or any other ordinary bird.

"It was a *big* bird," she said, "like a hawk, maybe. It shook the house."

Miraculously, the bird was not hurt, or at least not seriously. It dropped to the ground for a moment, then flew up, giving her a good opportunity to judge its wing span, which was almost equal to the width of the window.

"And that's six feet," she added. "I know, because I'd just measured it for drapes."

The bird did appear to be somewhat stunned. It flew up to a lamppost and perched there, shaking its head in a dazed fashion before flying off.

Mary Maichle knew that she had never seen such a bird before. Shocked as she was, she observed it carefully, noting the dark body, the white head, the hooked beak, and fierce eyes that looked—well, sort of eagle-like. She added rather apologetically, "Of course I've never seen an eagle. But is it possible?"

It was not only possible; it was unlikely that it could be anything *but* an adult bald eagle. To be sure, I asked the color of the tail.

"The same as the head," she said promptly. "White."

When I confirmed the identification, she was full of eager questions. Where had it come from? Was it migrating? And what was it doing in her back yard?

I wondered the same thing myself when she described her property in Potomac, with its generous plantings of ornamental shrubs and trees and without an open flyway. It was unlikely habitat for an eagle. But it was less than five miles from Great Falls, and I was immediately convinced that this was one of "my" eagles.

Actually, I have no right to claim the pair of eagles that chose to nest at Great Falls. I have never done anything for their benefit. But I have a proprietary feeling about them, a certain pride of discovery. We discovered them, Ted and I, on a Christmas Bird Count a few years ago, when it was rare enough to see even a single bald eagle. So the sight of the pair of them flying in tandem along the river near Violette's Lock was a matter of some excitement. A few weeks later, in early February, we stood at the Great Falls overlook and watched a pair of eagles—they had to be *our* eagles—building a nest on an island just above the falls, in full view of anyone who chose to watch.

We watched almost daily as the two flew over the treetops, snapping off sticks with their talons and placing them judiciously to construct a sturdy nest. We kept vigil when the female settled down on the nest and hoped fervently that she was sitting on viable eggs.

It had been 30 years since bald eagles had nested along the Potomac. Their alarming decline was ultimately attributed to their diet of fish contaminated with pesticides, which affected the birds' reproduction. The downward trend was reversed when DDT was banned, and eagles began a gradual comeback. We spent suspenseful weeks waiting to see if our eagles would produce young and rejoiced when two eaglets showed their fuzzy heads in the nest.

We watched the parents bring fish to share; we watched the youngsters make their first awkward flight from the nest. And we were there the next January to see the adults rehabilitate the old nest and occupy it again.

All this was of special interest to Mary Maichle, who had never dreamed she would see a bald eagle in the wild, much less on her own property.

Belatedly I thought to ask, "Did it break the window?"

She laughed. "No, but it sure scared my parakeets. Their cage is right by the window."

I was only joking when I suggested she might want to move the parakeets, but she wondered seriously if the eagle was after them. When I explained that bald eagles feed mainly on fish, she gave a gasp.

"My goldfish! Out in the pool!"

I didn't think our eagles would be interested in mere goldfish when they could get much bigger fish in the Potomac.

"Oh, but this is a pretty big goldfish," she said. "He's had the pool all to himself, and he's grown to about sixteen inches."

Curious, I offered to hold the phone while she went to check up on the goldfish. It was still there, she reported with some relief, and we continued to talk for a while about eagles in general and her visitor in particular. She felt honored and elated that her place had been chosen for a drop-in call, for whatever mysterious reason.

That still puzzled me, and I asked her to call back if she saw the eagle again.

That was in late November. I didn't hear from her again until mid-January. Her voice was almost as excited as it had been the first time I talked to her.

"Our friend came back!" she announced. "He ate the goldfish!"

She had caught him in the act, had watched him carry it off— and she had no regrets. She thought she understood at last the mystery of the November incident. The eagle, cruising over her house, had spotted the bright red of the goldfish in the pool— and had somehow miscalculated when he made a dive for it.

"He remembered!" she marveled. "After all this time, he remembered!"

I know of no research on the memory capacity of a bald eagle. But I know this one left behind a memory that will last a lifetime.

THE PRICE OF A SNOWY OWL

Dentists these days charge the full fee for a last-minute cancellation. Fair enough. But I should have canceled anyway. After all, how much is a snowy owl worth?

Unfortunately, the telephone call came just as I was ready to leave the house, and under pressure of time I made a poor decision.

The caller did not know me, and she did not know snowy owls. But she wanted to report that a large white owl was sitting on a 15th-floor window ledge directly across the street from her office in Virginia.

Identification was no problem; it was just my bad luck that her call came at such a critical moment.

It was a rainy day and the owl had been sitting there for some time, she said, showing no inclination to move. Anyone who wanted to see it could get a good view from her office window.

How could I pass up such an opportunity? But I was due at the dentist's office in ten minutes and, having been trained to treat dental appointments as moral imperatives, I made the decision automatically. But I did take time to make a quick call to Erika Wilson, who is always ready to drop everything to go in pursuit of a good bird. And this one was on her side of the river.

"I can be there in ten minutes!" she said briskly. And in ten minutes, I thought, I would be tilted back in the dentist's chair, suffering.

Such is the excitement stirred by the appearance of a snowy owl on the outskirts of the nation's capital that Erika had no problem filling her car with eager birders to accompany her on the afternoon jaunt. Later, when I was back home waiting for the effects of the novocaine to wear off, Erika called to give an ecstatic report. They had been treated to superb views of the owl (a life bird for her and two of her companions) and had taken a number of photographs, which she hoped would be good. So at least I might have yet another look at the picture of a snowy owl seen by others.

As for the owl itself, the latest word was that it had flown from its perch at about the time the evening rush hour started. And that was the last word. Another chance at a snowy owl had been missed. Timing is everything.

If this had been a life bird for me, I would have felt worse about it. Actually, I had seen three snowy owls in my lifetime, but I had missed far more than I had seen.

I consoled myself with memories of the one I had seen, white on white, against the snow in a Pennsylvania farm field where a sober young Amish boy had pointed it out. I thought of the one I saw alight on a parapet at Ft. McHenry in Baltimore, where "The Star-Spangled Banner" was created.

The third was only a half-sighting, not a long, satisfying view. Driving around the Capital Beltway on a winter day, I joked to Ted, "I'm looking for a snowy owl," knowing that one had been reported in the general area. The words had scarcely left my mouth when I followed up with, "And there it is!"

At 55 miles per hour, we got a fleeting glimpse of a great white owl being pursued by a mob of crows. By the time we reached the next exit and circled back for a closer look, owl and crows had disappeared. We wasted the next hour cruising all the side streets in a vain search.

Vain searches characterize too many of my experiences with snowy owls. They appear here irregularly, in winters when a shortage of lemmings on the arctic tundra forces them to range far south of their accustomed habitat in search of food. Here, instead of rocky cliffs, they find high-rise buildings that serve just as well, especially if those buildings are located near an open space where rodents are easy prey.

The Mall in downtown Washington is just the right kind of

place. One year a snowy owl was seen repeatedly on buildings fronting the Mall, including the Washington Monument. But he was not seen by me.

The one that perched for days on a church steeple in Cambridge, Maryland, stayed around until the day we were free to make the trip across the Chesapeake Bay to pay our respects. It took off a half-hour before we arrived.

And then there was the one that was reported sitting on a utility pole in a back yard in Arlington, Virginia, just across the Potomac—a short hop for me. Unfortunately, I had an appointment with a senator that day, and senators, like dentists, must not be kept waiting. The best I could do was to get an early start and detour through Arlington on my way to Capitol Hill. I spent as much time as I dared in the neighborhood where the owl had been seen, questioning sharp-eyed youngsters on their way to school in case any of them had spotted it.

Time was against me. Forced to abandon the hunt, I hurried on to the Senate Office Building, where I spent the morning in serious discussion, trying not to think of owls.

Next morning, I found the elusive owl staring at me from the front page of *The Washington Post*. The photograph had been taken on the roof of the Senate Office Building, where the owl had been sitting all the while I was in conference, just two floors below.

After the 15th-floor owl, I got a second chance. Snowy owls were being reported from various points: in Maryland, in Virginia, in Delaware. The most dependable one was being seen regularly by local farmers and birders along the entrance road to Bombay Hook National Wildlife Refuge in Delaware. It had arrived in early December, found the hunting good, and stayed on. Birders who made the trip to Bombay Hook saw the bird from the road, sometimes sitting out in a stubblefield, sometimes perched on a barn, a silo, or a utility pole.

"You can't miss it," friends assured us as we set off for the two-and-a-half-hour drive.

"Want to bet?" I said, with well-earned cynicism. But with hand-drawn maps furnished by well-wishers and generous notes that included even the names on mailboxes, we were cautiously hopeful.

It was all predictable. We spent a good hour (or rather, a bad hour) driving up and down farm roads, pausing at frequent intervals to scan the fields and farm buildings for a splotch of white.

Nothing.

Disheartened, we drove into the refuge and made a stop at the visitors center, hoping that some of the refuge personnel could offer a clue. No one was in sight. All hands were out on patrol, and the office was closed.

Debating the next step, we returned to the car.

A young woman in a pickup truck pulled up beside us and called out, "Have you seen the snowy owl?"

Miraculously, she wasn't asking us where it was; she was ready to tell us—with exact directions.

"It's sitting on the peak of the barn roof, behind the red brick house with the wrought-iron fence. It's been there all morning. It's a beauty!"

We were off.

No one answered our knock at the red brick house so, without the usual permission, we dared to drive past it toward the barn where the owl sat placidly like an ornament, undisturbed by the ever-so-gradual approach of the car. As we crept closer, a yard at a time, I kept my binoculars on the magnificent bird, observing every detail of the delicate black edging on his feathers, the faint sprinkling of black on the crown, the fuzz of whiskers around his beak, the golden eyes that opened and stared as we came nearer.

He was sleeping, and we disturbed him. Ted at the wheel, his camera at the ready, edged ever closer, taking pictures from the car window at each advance.

At the first click of the shutter, the owl turned his head and stared straight at the photographer. Then, in an attitude of noble indifference, he turned his head and tucked his beak into a pillow of white feathers, highlighted by the sun.

Forward . . . click! Forward . . . click! Seldom does a photographer find so cooperative a subject.

Annoyed at last by the repeated noise, the great bird raised his head, gave us a golden stare, and lifted his wings for take-off. But it was just too much bother. Instead of flying away, he simply settled farther down on the slope of the roof and there he sat, blinking sleepily.

"Come on, Ted. We have plenty of pictures. Let's let him sleep."

In a euphoric haze, we retreated down the lane. Looking back, we saw that the owl had returned to his initial perch on the peak of the barn roof, monarch of all he surveyed. That was the picture we would carry with us all the way home.

"Ka-THUD! Ka-THUD! Ka-THUD!"

An ominous noise punctured our euphoria, bringing us back to the real world with all its pitfalls for innocent travelers. Somewhere, beneath the solemn stare of the snowy owl, we had run over a lethal object that had inflicted terminal damage on a new tire.

It had been a long time since either of us had changed a tire. But no help was in sight, so we had no choice. We tackled the challenge gamely, grateful for the step-by-step guidance in the owner's manual—and thankful as well for the soothing presence of the great white owl, which made the whole ordeal seem worth-while.

A SCENE FROM HITCHCOCK

Standing at the mouth of a cave, we peered in at two fuzzy, ungainly chicks. They were very young vultures, still wobbly and uncoordinated. There was nothing ominous about them except for the guttural hisses they directed at us. But they brought to mind a telephone call I'd answered earlier in the year when spring was only a promise.

The message on my answering machine was the eeriest one it has ever recorded. The voice was that of a farm woman across the county line to the north. She gave the name Judy Alden, and urgently requested that I call her back.

Her question concerned turkey vultures. She had 30 or 40 of them in her barnyard—riding on the backs of her sheep. Should she be worried? And after that question she added a postscript: "It's getting near lambing time—that's why I'm concerned."

There was a time when I would not have been concerned— merely intrigued—by the specter of vultures riding sheep-back, believing that these are harmless birds that feed only on dead carcasses. But within the past year I had been reading in the county newspaper a series of gruesome accounts narrating farmers' experiences with vultures attacking, and even killing, livestock.

Having grown up in farm country where tall tales were an acknowledged art form, I read the stories with proper skepticism. As the stories proliferated, my skepticism only increased. It was like a wave of hysteria; one tale spawned another, even worse. No reporter had ever witnessed the macabre scenes. All were based on farmers' hearsay. I was ready to write them off as myths—until I encountered an article by an enterprising reporter who had interviewed a veterinarian on the subject.

It was true, he said. Vultures had become more aggressive of late. While they were not known to attack healthy livestock, they would gang up on a defenseless cow that was down with undulant fever. And he knew of more than one instance of vultures preying on cows as they were giving birth—attacking both cow and calf with deadly results. His eyewitness testimony was sickeningly realistic.

I made haste to call Judy Alden to tell her yes, indeed, she should be worried for the safety of her ewes, which must be giving out an aroma that attracted opportunistic vultures.

Wisely, she had not waited for my return call. She had already taken steps, calling state government offices for help. After numerous referrals from office to office, she finally reached a person in the Department of Natural Resources who was not only authoritative but interested. He had dealt with such cases before.

"Scare them away and get your ewes into the barn," he counseled. "Make noise. Fire a shotgun." Then, surprised at her reply: "You don't *have* a shotgun? You live on a farm, and you don't have a shotgun?"

Once he'd absorbed that incredible truth, he was helpful and decisive.

"I'll be right out," he said. And by the time I reached the caller, he had come and gone, dispersing the vultures with noisemakers and leaving her a supply in the event of further appearances.

"It was a relief to see them leave," Judy admitted. "I'm not superstitious, and I don't have any hang-ups about vultures. But I swear, it was like a scene from a Hitchcock movie. Remember *The Birds*, where they terrorized a whole town?"

I did remember. Hitchcock's birds, as I recalled, were crows. He would have done well to use vultures instead. They look far more sinister.

Later, I talked with a wildlife biologist who had made a special study of vultures.

"Those weren't turkey vultures," he asserted positively. "They don't attack live animals. It's black vultures that do that."

Predicting that there would be more incidents involving vultures raiding barnyards, he said, "Their population is increasing, and they're getting more competitive, more aggressive."

• • •

The fuzzy chicks we watched staggering drunkenly inside the dim cave were part of the population explosion. These were little black vultures, already making menacing noises. But they were awkward and inept at this stage. It was hard to believe that, within a few months, they might be players in a macabre scene worthy of Hitchcock.

✛

RESTLESS ROBINS
AND A LOST HUMMINGBIRD

No two winters are alike, in weather or in birdlife. Among my most memorable winters is the one that was punctuated by telephone calls from Sam Pancake, reporting on the welfare of his errant hummingbird.

It was a rufous hummingbird that had strayed far from its western habitat and found a hospitable spot in Sam's garden, in the quiet community of Takoma Park just outside Washington, D.C. Arriving in November, long after all the summer ruby-throats had departed, it showed no inclination to move on. When the last of the flowers in Sam's colorful garden had withered, it relied on the sugar-water he provided, to which he added a protein supplement when the weather grew colder and insects were hard to find. By the ingenious use of a heating pad, he kept the sugar-water from freezing. At night the bird took shelter in the dense ivy growing up the chimney wall.

Naturally, the bird was newsworthy. Birders came flocking from six states to add this rarity to their life lists (or state lists). A licensed bander came, captured the wanderer to verify its species and sex, and released it with a tiny aluminum band on its leg carrying an identification number that would help trace its wanderings if it was ever recaptured elsewhere. Articles were written in ornithological journals reporting on the incidence of rufous hummingbirds in the east.

And then, suddenly, interest shifted as another bird became newsworthy—this time not a rare bird, but the familiar American robin. Nor was it in this case a single bird, but hundreds of the species—and in early February, when people don't expect to see robins in Maryland.

All day my telephone rang. It started before breakfast when my friend Mary Ellen, who lives less than a mile away, called and said, "You're not going to believe this, but I have a hundred robins in my back yard!"

I did believe it, but I had a hard time convincing her that wintering robins are not uncommon in our area. True, they aren't usually seen in back yards, but are seen instead in secluded woodland tracts where they have shelter and an abundance of berry-producing plants for nourishment. In one of our favorite haunts, we could depend on finding a flock numbering 200 or more at any time throughout the winter.

"But the ground is frozen!" Mary Ellen protested. "How can they live?"

Certainly not on worms. I explained that robins, like other birds, adjust their diet to match the season. Often, when they have exhausted the supply of wild berries, they go on restless quests for more food sources and descend on back yards planted with attractive ornamentals—pyracantha, holly, crab apples, and the like. All these Mary Ellen had in abundance, so her yard was favored by this winter visitation.

But it was not only her yard. Suburbanites in every direction went out to pick up their morning papers and saw robins. Flocks and flocks of robins. Never had so many been reported. Some were reported directly to me by people who had my number. Others were reported to the Audubon Society, where phone lines were overloaded as soon as the offices opened. Still more were reported to newspapers and television stations. And inevitably, the reports were accompanied by questions:

"What's going on? What does it mean?"

By mid-morning I was hoarse from repeating explanations:

Yes, robins do stay in the area all winter—precisely how many we don't know, but we always see them on Christmas Bird Counts.

No, cold weather doesn't do them in, as long as they have an adequate and accessible supply of berries. Heavy snows that bury the supply or ice storms that glaze everything are the big risks.

No, it is not uncommon for flocks to wander about in the winter. It happens every few years, usually in January or February. But yes, it is uncommon to see them in such numbers. In all my years of birding in this area, I have never seen so many.

Weathermen and meteorologists from all the television stations checked in with all the usual questions. They were especially interested in statistics from previous years, a healthy sign of scientific curiosity. And then they disappointed me with the utterly unscientific question:

"Does this mean an early spring?"

Come on, guys! You're the meteorologists! You tell me if we're going to have an early spring!

The truth is, no one knew what these unprecedented numbers meant. It did, indeed, seem unlikely that all these were "local" flocks. It was much more likely that there had been an influx of outsiders—whether from the north or the south, we did not know. When observations were reported and analyzed, we might learn what had impelled all these robins to go walkabout in mid-winter—whether it was an adverse weather pattern of which we were then unaware or a food shortage elsewhere.

Speculation at that point was useless. I was willing to predict that it would be a short-lived phenomenon, that within a few days the flocks would disappear overnight as mysteriously as they had appeared, that winter would spin out its allotted days, and that the proverbial "first robin" of spring would arrive on seasonal schedule.

Meanwhile, we could all enjoy this stimulating diversion, a brief reprieve from the winter doldrums.

As predicted, the robins departed for parts unknown before the week came to an end.

And Sam Pancake, who had not seen a single vagrant robin, called to report that his rufous hummingbird was still in residence. He was confident, now, that it would survive the winter.

✜
FULL CIRCLE

Another cycle of the seasons is closing as the lengthening days of February merge gently into spring. There is a satisfaction in the sameness of the cycle, repeated each year. But the excitement lies in the knowledge that this spring will not be the same as last spring, and that there will be fresh surprises ahead.

An editorial in *The Washington Post* bemoans the miserable days of winter and the "silences of February." The writer could not have visited the same woods that I visited these last few days, when I found them far from silent.

The orchestra is tuning up, and the soloists are rehearsing. In *my* woods, the cardinals are singing their uninhibited aria to spring—and to lady cardinals. Blue jays are gathering in great numbers as they did last fall, screaming to one another and the world at large of news that has escaped our attention. Overhead, flocks of businesslike crows caw on their way to work and, from a nearby thicket, a song sparrow trills sweetly.

Off in the woods, a pileated woodpecker knocks vigorously on wood, and a titmouse whistles the same two notes over and over, as if calling a lost dog. A pair of doves, seated side by side on a cedar bough, exchange notes that are considered mournful by everyone but doves. Echoes of "Bob White! Bob White!" announce the presence of quail in the cornfield beyond the woods. The calls are interrupted by the first half of an early meadowlark's song.

There is a busyness about the woods these days. Robins are massing forces in treetops, getting ready to descend on city lawns and earthworms. Their voices are soft, but they are not silent. Roving gangs of cedar waxwings fill the air with their high, thin "zee-zee-zee" as they dash about on their endless gourmet tour. Chickadees dart through the trees, buzzing noisily. Flocks of juncos feed ravenously on the ground or flit among the lower branches. Squirrels chatter and make a great business of gathering dry leaves for nesting material.

If you visit the swamps, you will hear the red-winged blackbirds practicing a few tentative notes. Their cousins, the grackles, are already clucking overhead as they return by the thousands from their southern vacation-lands. *They* have no complaint about February in the Washington area. But even as the grackles return, other residents who think of this as "the South" are preparing to leave us.

That is my complaint with February: not that it is "miserable" or "silent," but that it is sad. It is the month of leave-taking and departures. Last week there were canvasbacks and goldeneyes on the Georgetown Reservoir and an armada of ruddy ducks on the Potomac below National Airport. Today they are all gone. Along Chesapeake Bay, the tundra swans are forming not-so-silent squadrons to take off for the far north. Their voices and the beat of their great wings fill the air. Along the Eastern Shore, the numbers of snow geese are dwindling, and hundreds of thousands of Canada geese are making departing noises.

I know that the swamps will soon echo with the voices of thousands of peeper frogs, and that the woods will be filled with the songs of thrushes and warblers. But it is sad to think of the voices that will not be heard, and of the stillness that will fall over the winter haunts of the great water birds whose stay with us is all too brief.

Silence does not reign at home. Now is the time to review recordings of warbler songs, in preparation for the coming invasion. The telephone rings with welcome interruptions, each call an invitation—to solve a mystery, to make a new friend, to embark on an adventure, to pursue a new line of avian research, or simply to share in the joys of discovery.

ACKNOWLEDGMENTS

Many of the chapters included in this book are adapted from my column, "Notes from Melody Lane," published in the *Audubon Naturalist News*. My thanks go to its editor, Kathy Rushing, with whom I have enjoyed not only a rewarding professional relationship but a warm friendship. The same is true of Mary Bowers, editor of *Bird Watcher's Digest*, in which several of the chapters appeared. Greg Linder, my editor at NorthWord Press, deserves high marks for creativity in giving the book its title, and for his sound editorial judgment, tempered with endless patience and tact, which has made the publication process an uncommonly happy experience.

Family members never expect thanks for doing what comes naturally, and I won't embarrass them with effusions of gratitude for their understanding and support. But it is only fair to note that my husband Ted and son Steve had a major part in this effort. Ted is my sounding board, my critic-in-residence. Without his steadfast encouragement, I would never have begun this book. And without Steve's gentle nagging, I would probably never have finished it. Lyme Disease forced me to put it aside for a full year and, in recovery, I lacked the will to pick it up again. But Steve, who had learned at an early age that writers do better when faced with deadlines, gave me a target date for completion—and held me to it. So this book is theirs as much as it is mine.

—Lola Oberman